The SNUGGLE Party GUIDEBOOK

Create Deeper Friendships, Decrease Loneliness, & Enjoy Nurturing Touch Community

Dave Wheitner

foreword by James "Jas" Davis, drawings by
Kristen Reynolds, games co-authored with Amy Baker

First Paperback Edition
Divergent Drummer Publications
Portland, Oregon

ISBN: 978-0-9817764-7-7

Library of Congress Control Number: 2014912766
Library of Congress subject headings:
Family & Relationships—Friendship
Reference—Personal & Practical Guides

Inquiries and information: davewheitner.com

Divergent Drummer Publications
Portland, Oregon

Version 1.2

Praise for
The Snuggle Party Guidebook

Indie Book Awards Finalist, Relationships

~Praise from Experts~

"Far more than an excellent and thorough guidebook. It is an inspirational work that opens delightful pathways to intimacy with oneself and others. I loved how it offers healing from limiting stereotypical gender roles, and the accompanying photos always brought a smile to my face. Don't miss this book!"

Karla Baur, M.S.W., sex therapist and co-author of *Our Sexuality*, the best-selling college textbook

"As a Professional Cuddler, I am so proud of the concepts of non-sexual touch in this book. With the tools here anyone can master touch and improve their life in a simple but profound way."

Samantha Hess, founder of Cuddle Up to Me, author of *Touch: The Power of Human Connection*

"Want more friendly nurturing touch in your life? Dave's book can show you how to get started—and Dave, can I come to one of your snuggle parties?"

Dr. Betty Martin, Cuddle Party board member & facilitator, author of *Touch: Receiving, Giving, Taking, Allowing* (forthcoming)

"An easy to use guidebook on how to run snuggle events as well as a gentle description of the importance of touch for all of us. I recommend it highly!"

Virgil Cater, R.N., founder of Opening to Love, event facilitator, Certified Spiritual Sexual Educator, Certified Tantric Educator

"I'm convinced that our culture's explosion of addiction is directly tied to a massive shortage of opportunities for consensual and loving touch. *Snuggle Party* is simply code for *pop-up clinic for the soul.*"

Buster Ross, MA, AASECT Certified Sexuality Counselor

~Praise from Other Readers and Reviewers~

"I believe this book is on the leading edge of a quiet revolution in how people relate to one another."

K.A. Klepper

"It thoroughly covers the issues over which I had overt or subconscious concerns. I especially appreciated the section on consent, which offered me vocabulary for knowing what I want and how to get just that. Absolutely 5 stars."

Anna Reedy

"I was struck by how simple the author makes it all, laying out all the planning details in easy to follow ways. I would highly recommend this book if you or anyone you know is looking for ways to connect more deeply with your friends."

A. Crockett

"Exactly what I needed! I've heard of this concept, and wanted to start something up in my area. The perfect step-by-step guide to creating a healthy and safe environment for adding more touch into our lives. An easy read, interspersed with humor and cute drawings, and flows nicely."

"Jaye"

"The practices and way of being that are presented in this book...have impacted my life greatly and helped to open me to connection and courage."

F. Joseph Von Hoven

Contents

Foreword

These pages provide instruction on how to host gatherings where participants share playful and nurturing touch, and in the process learn vital skills for getting their basic touch needs met in healthy, caring ways. While that may sound odd, the truth is that our society desperately needs this book. We live in a touch-phobic culture, yet the research over the past several decades is conclusive: Human beings are social creatures designed by nature to thrive when we regularly experience physical affection.

Our species needs good nurturing touch in order to be healthy and happy. Good touch helps to regulate our nervous systems, strengthens our immunity, bonds us together as community, and contributes to our overall vitality. Yet while sharing nurturing touch is natural, we live in a culture that has created so much fear around touch that what is completely natural is no longer "normal." In 2002, a group called LoveTribe started hosting "Snuggle Parties" in Portland, Oregon, with the intention of creating more heart-conscious, touch-positive communities and culture. Within a decade, thousands of people in dozens of cities attended our events, and numerous individuals and groups sprang up across the country engaged in similar work.

Dave Wheitner is one of those transformational leaders. In this book, he shares how he came to host such gatherings, and then walks us through the steps of creating our own touch-positive events and how to handle various issues that may arise. He also provides resources, including ideas for intention setting and leveling exercises. Along the way, he shares the words of numerous participants who have experienced and/or helped to create these events. The importance of this book cannot be overstated, because while snuggle gatherings are certainly fun and rejuvenating, they also contribute to the health of individuals, our relationships, and the planet.

We all need human contact, and our personal relationships (or lack thereof) are not always enough to fill that need. The more touch is lacking in our life, the more our bodies crave it. It's not something we want–like a car. It is something we need, like oxygen and water. Babies die if they do not get human touch, and adults rarely live full, healthy, happy lives without it. Few of us realize that we are surrounded by people with similar needs for affection. We are like the man in Dante's Hell, standing chin deep in water and unable to drink, because our culture has conflated "nurturing touch" with "sexual touch" so much that it can feel dangerous to share affection with anyone with whom we don't want to be sexual.

While it may sound simplistic, gatherings where we share nurturing touch directly address our bodies' needs for connection beneath the level of our self-consciousness. Our bodies are where we meet the world and where our impressions of the world arise and reside. It is in our bodies that we feel anxiety, fear, and pain as well as desire, joy, acceptance, and love. When we get enough nurturing, playful touch, we experience a greater sense of sufficiency, expansiveness, abundance, and well-being, and we feel more connected with others and the world as a whole. We are healthier, less fearful, and more open to engaging in community and sharing/conserving resources–essential qualities for living more sustainably.

With this book, Dave Wheitner helps lead the charge to create communal opportunities for meeting our shared needs for healthy touch, and in so doing, reclaim the commons of our sensuality as a powerful way to improve our individual and collective physical health, emotional happiness, material well-being, international security, and ecological sustainability. This is a book that will change the world for the better.

James "Jas" Davis
Founder, LoveTribe
Co-Founder, Organic Relating

Puppy Pile Peace on Earth

1 About This Book—and What's a Snuggle Party?

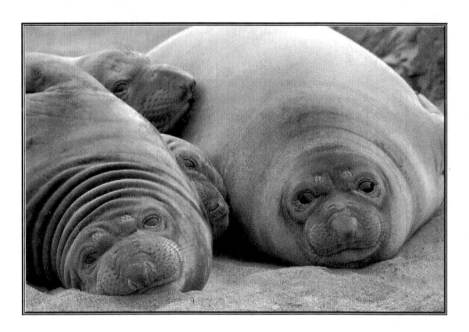

"Snuggling has brought to me more intimate friendships and stronger community. I grew up in a small town where I would see the same people fairly frequently, but I never felt the same level of closeness as I do with this group of people I'm actually bonding with physically. Physical touch drives deeper into my psyche that these people really like me."

—*K. R., age 51*

Imagine waking up one morning in the near future, and realizing that several profound changes have occurred in your life:

- You enjoy deeper connections with others.

- You experience greater intimacy and less loneliness.

- You resonate with more friends on a heartfelt level, not just on an intellectual or conversational level.

- Social settings and gatherings don't feel so superficial.

- Physical affection is readily available beyond romantic and sexual relationships.

- Relationships are no longer "all-or-nothing" when it comes to nourishing physical touch. You've found a refreshing middle ground between platonic friends who share little or no physical contact, and romantic connections who share all types of contact.

- You're better at saying "Yes" to what you really want and "No" to what you don't want, while empowering others around you to do the same.

- Your romantic relationships or dates are no longer so overshadowed by touch-related "neediness."

- You're helping to create a healthier, more integrated, holistic, and sustainable understanding of how touch and connectedness function in our lives.

These are some pretty fun things to imagine, aren't they? If you desire some of the changes above, you're not alone. And you've come to the right place. As you'll learn from my own exciting journey, experiencing some these changes has led me to appreciate snuggle parties tremendously.

If you don't consider yourself a super-snuggly person, but just want a bit more positive touch, you're not alone, either. For much of my own life, I've actually been relatively shy about things like snuggling and hugging. I still am in many situations, and I still have a lot to learn about this stuff myself. I don't strive to make myself into a super-snuggly person. But since I've become a bit more open about touch, and a bit more comfortable around other people who are, I've also become happier.

This book is designed to empower you to create successful touch-positive events that include snuggling. You'll have the tools to do this right in your own living room or neighborhood. If you're new to snuggling and want to get started by simply inviting over a few friends, you'll probably be ready after just a few hours with this book. If you aim to create larger or more public events, or to create a group devoted to regular snuggles, you'll appreciate the finer details.

The pages ahead will give you the following knowledge:

- what snuggle parties are, and how they can positively impact your life and others' lives
- how to recruit participants and get them more comfortable with snuggling
- how to set up physical and emotional environments that are safe and comfortable—both for your snuggle party participants, and for you

- how to anticipate and manage social and psychological dynamics you might encounter, including tips for addressing sexuality, gender, and couples/dating topics
- how to approach money, volunteer, and other resource needs if they arise, in ways that help you to take care of yourself
- concepts and resources relevant to other snuggle activities like one-on-one snuggling, cuddle coaching or consulting, snuggle therapy, and the like, should you wish to branch out in other directions

I believe that snuggle parties have the power to change your life, because they profoundly changed mine after just a few events. As you'll see, they helped me through one of the most challenging periods of my life. And I believe they have the power to change the world, because I've discovered socially cutting-edge communities who are energized by such gatherings. I believe these events can help to address issues such as loneliness, aging, prejudice, depression, and violence.

Touch-positive activities like snuggling may even be a foundational cornerstone of economic sustainability. As I discuss in *Naked Idealism*, an empowerment guide for socially conscious people, quests for materialistic goods are sometimes vain attempts to obtain more intimacy. For example, we might believe that a large house or a bright red convertible is going to attract a loving mate, not realizing that there are much easier—and much more direct—ways to attract intimacy. As Bob Czimbal, co-author of *Vitamin T: A Guide to Healthy Touch*, puts it, "When we have a sense of belonging, we don't need belongings so much." Society doesn't often teach us such things, and that's where you and I enter the picture.

A number of forward-thinking, deeply caring individuals have been leading this movement for years, often modestly, and largely under the radar of mainstream culture. I was very fortunate to discover them after life crises motivated me to open my mind. Because these wonderful people have been so helpful to me, I'm eager to help share their gifts and knowledge with you.

As I continued to meet talented facilitators and thinkers, and attend additional events, I realized that my education in various aspects of psychology offers a perfect lens for deeper perspective. This book is my attempt to combine others' most important ideas about snuggle parties with my own, in a way that is useful to you.

I aim to inspire you, to provide you with a wealth of useful tools and perspectives, to empower you to create many wonderful connections. I do not intend to replace professional facilitators or existing organizations that offer paid facilitator trainings. Those have a valuable place for individuals who have the resources and desire to access them. I want to equip you to get started on your own as soon as possible, with a minimal initial investment of time and money.

This all aligns with a larger vision: a world in which everyone everywhere experiences an abundance of healthy, nurturing touch. This community touch movement can happen if people around the globe, including you, are empowered to create connective events in their homes and neighborhoods.

To ensure we're on the same page before going any further, let's define a snuggle party:

A snuggle party is an event where participants share consensual, nurturing touch. Everyone is clothed, and the event is non-sexual. The energy is intended to be relaxing and soothing, rather than arousing or stimulating. Touch might include holding hands, exchanging back, shoulder, or foot massage, light facial touch, holding, playing with hair, or spooning. Open communication is emphasized. This includes stating one's own needs and boundaries, as well as asking for permission. More boisterous activities at snuggle parties can include playful wrestling, puppy piles (many people blissfully snuggled together), and pillow fights.[1]

Organizers have used terms such as *cuddles, snuggles, cuddle gatherings, snuggle gatherings, snuggle parties,* and

cuddle piles. Roughly a year after the first organized U.S. snuggles appeared in Portland, Oregon, through a group later known as LoveTribe, a New York company garnered press for its independently developed and trademarked "Cuddle Party" model.[2] Because I respect the work taken to develop that specific brand, I use non-trademarked phrases including *snuggle party* here. As there are still millions of people to reach, my hope is that more voices and approaches will reach a much larger overall audience. No one school of thought is necessarily more "correct" than others.

While snuggling can be included in events that also allow more sexual touch, many in this heart-conscious, touch-positive movement would call any event with sexual touch something other than a *snuggle party*. That is my recommendation as well.[3]

You will find a wealth of information in the following chapters. However, you don't need to master everything for your first few events, especially if you're starting small with just a few friends. You may never need some of the information at all. For the most part, snuggles are relatively simple, relaxed events, but I want you to be prepared for the most challenging possibilities as well.

It's like being the pilot of a plane, where you and your passengers will be more confident if you're prepared for a range of scenarios. Alongside "basic flight procedures" that apply to most snuggle journeys, there are also adjustments for when you want to fly over somewhat different territory, and tips for the rare situations when the often-demonstrated oxygen mask or under-seat flotation device might actually be necessary. Of course, you will be traveling in much greater comfort, spaciousness, and style, snuggling up on soft padding, pillows, and blankets.

I'll be very transparent and up front about a few things. First, this book does not promise an effortless overnight quick fix to everything. However, if you're willing to put in just a bit of regular effort over the next few months, and to do it with an openness to fun and possibility, you'll likely experience many of the wonderful, life-enhancing benefits that other snugglers and I have.

In other words, you'll transform from a *snuggle-not* into a *snugglenaut*, venturing into new galaxies of connection.

Secondly, I don't pretend to have it all together myself. I still often hesitate, or fail to act at all, due to fear of rejection. This may happen when I want to deepen a friendship, ask someone to snuggle, or even ask someone to dance. I avoid putting myself fully out there, falling into the all-too-human trap of secretly rejecting someone before they have a chance to reject me. I still feel lonely sometimes, and I still have plenty of inner work to do on how I relate to myself and others.

I've met many people who seem much more extroverted and touchy-feely than I am—people for whom an abundance of physical touch seems to come more naturally and effortlessly. I'm not one of those people. While I'm sometimes very social, I'm probably about average on the "social touch comes naturally" front.

Despite the above, snuggle events have already taken me a few steps beyond where I was before, and beyond what I previously thought was possible. I've experienced deeper heartfelt connections with a number of people. This is great news for you, because it means this stuff can work even for those of us who weren't born with a super-social-snuggle gene. (If you *are* one of those people, it will be especially exciting to see how you put this book's information and tools to use.)

I invite you to give yourself a big hug for coming this far. Seriously, take a second. I'm not going anywhere.

Before moving ahead, we have a bit of homework. So I don't scare you away, I'll clarify that a bit: *optional but recommended, and fun* homework!

The questions on the following ideasheet will help you to clarify why you want to throw snuggle parties, and to begin thinking about what you want them to look like. Your answers don't need to be lengthy or perfect, but spending some time on them will help you to have the best party possible. Should you run into any obstacles along the way, your answers will also help to keep you motivated, excited, and focused on what's most important to you.

You may want to return to the ideasheet after reading the next few chapters, when you'll have even more ideas about the benefits of snuggle parties. You can download a printable version of the ideasheet and other goodies you'll find later in the book at snuggleparty.org.

Snuggle Party Visioning Ideasheet #1

What are your top three reasons for wanting to host snuggle parties?

What short-term positive changes (within 2 months) do you anticipate from snuggle parties?

What longer-term positive changes do you anticipate from snuggle parties?

How may snuggle parties positively impact other areas of your life?

Areas can include physical, emotional, and spiritual well-being; relationships with friends, family, and existing or potential romantic partner(s); finances; work and career; and anything else that comes to mind.

2   How I Discovered the Power of Snuggle Parties

"I grew up in a hands-off, touch-deprived atmosphere. Snuggling changed my life. Attending and facilitating snuggle events, I met my partner, made wonderful friends, and helped create heart-centered, touch positive community. Snuggling helped me realize I was lovable, worthy of giving and receiving loving human touch."

—*S. S., age 40*

During life's most turbulent times, when the pain can seem almost unbearable, we can have the most profound breakthroughs.

Just a few years ago, this book could not have happened. Many of the soul-shifting events I've attended and life-transforming people I've met would have seemed far too eccentric or "woo-woo" for me. I had long been concerned about improving societal well-being, but primarily through a very heady, cerebral lens. I had worked hard to earn an Ivy League degree, to earn two graduate degrees with honors, and to complete advanced life coach training so I could work with clients on a range of topics. Spending several months of my life researching and writing about something like "snuggle parties" would have seemed absurd.

Additionally, because I grew up receiving and witnessing nurturing physical touch more than many kids probably do, I took such things for granted. From an early age through my elementary school years, my mom tucked me into bed at night and rubbed my back while saying prayers with me. I sometimes spotted my parents hugging each other or sharing a kiss as I entered a room. I recall my dad and other relatives sometimes giving me hugs or pats on the back when greeting me, or when congratulating me for an accomplishment. However, like many kids, I focused too much on what my family *didn't* have (in our case, we had relatively limited financial resources), and too little on what we *did* have.

During college, I met a wonderful woman with whom I fell deeply in love, and we married a few years later. As many people do, I felt certain that we'd grow old together. For more than 15 years, I enjoyed the comfort of relying upon her for the vast majority of my physical affection needs.

Then, a major midlife crisis changed everything. I was forced to look at my own life, and at the reality of our culture, even more squarely in the face.

My partner and I began to realize that we had some major incompatibilities. This included fundamental differences in physical affection needs that hadn't been apparent when we first met. We talked seriously about the possibility of separating. Because we loved each other in many ways, I desperately sought creative ways to make things work, even when approaches such as counseling left us with little hope.

Although I already had degrees in psychology and counseling, I pored through many additional books on relationships and intimacy. I consulted with people who had explored alternative ways of structuring relationships. I sought out events that stretched my boundaries.

My exploration included flying across the U.S., from Pittsburgh, PA to Portland, OR, to attend the first Ecosex Symposium. Its focus upon the linkages between human relationships and global sustainability (social, environmental, and economic) fascinated me. What I encountered there drew me out of my head and into my body much more. I experienced several sensual but non-sexual workshops where participants exchanged nourishing physical touch, in safe spaces created by skilled facilitators.

These experiences were quite exciting, and they marked a few critical turning points for me. For one, this was the first time in nearly 17 years that I had substantially exchanged affectionate physical touch beyond brief hugs or handshakes with anyone other than my partner. Doing so had felt taboo, a major no-no, almost akin to cheating. Secondly, they marked the beginning of my exposure to many fascinating outside-the-box people, versed in a variety of connective body, mind, and spirit integration practices. These included Tantra, Ecstatic Dance, various forms of mindfulness meditation and rituals, and snuggling.

A few months after the symposium, I contacted Stara Shakti, an organizer I had met. She and her partner Jack Ohana had recently co-founded a group now called Oregon Touch. It was devoted to events such as snuggles and massage trades. I was eager to learn how I might duplicate such events in Pittsburgh. Stara and others in the group kindly allowed me to Skype into their next planning meeting. The discussions about various types of events opened my mind even more.

These experiences inspired me to attend a Network for a New Culture retreat in the snowy mountains of beautiful West Virginia, just a few hours from Pittsburgh. There I experienced my first snuggle party, with a small group of people I had known for only a day or two. I initially felt awkward, but as I relaxed into it I experienced a blend of connection and happiness that is difficult to describe in words. I also experienced the power of other simple but profound connective techniques, such as eye gazing and synchronized breathing, and a "sensual feast" in which we slowly and deliberately fed one another desserts and other delicious foods. I left that long weekend with the same broadened sense of connection and possibility that I had felt after my trip to Portland.

Back at home, however, the connection that felt most important to me was not destined to continue. At least not in its existing form. While we loved each other a great deal, my partner and I agreed that our differences were too great for us to continue relating in the same way. As I approached age 40, I would soon be separated from the person I had relied on for the vast majority of my physical intimacy needs—and many other intimacy needs—for nearly half of my life.

Along with being deeply sad about leaving my partner and a wonderful foster daughter we had co-parented for two years, I was incredibly scared. It was by far one of the most challenging times of my entire life. However, my recent connective experiences had given me a ray of hope. There were additional ways to connect with others, to feel supported.

After much deliberation, intensive therapy, and coaching, I decided I would move to Portland to begin a new phase of life. Then many things began to happen rapidly. Around this time, Stara posted an ad for a housemate. Coincidentally, I had already seen the room, as it was the same one they had Skyped me into for the planning meeting several weeks earlier! After another talk with Stara and her housemate, everything was set to go.

Just a few weeks later, I was three time zones away from the region where I had spent my entire life. Amidst a mix of emotions, it was a massive shift for me. I had given up many of the material belongings and human connections with which I had previously identified myself. Each night during my first week in Portland, I struggled to fall asleep on a camping pad in my basement room. As I watched the cold winter drizzle through the window, I feared going crazy.

Given the nature of our differences, my partner and I had briefly attempted an open relationship, where we could each see other people. During that time, I had met someone in Portland whom I was now able to see several times per week. Although she was very affectionate, warm, and loving, I struggled when we didn't see each other for a few days in a row, and I experienced little or no touch. She had a busy schedule, and was still dating a few other people at that time.

We had mutually agreed to this arrangement beforehand, but it ended up being more challenging than I had anticipated. Even though I never find myself bored during "alone" time, I had to find other ways to meet some of my touch needs. While I now had housemates, I was no longer living with a romantic partner. Being under an exceptional amount of stress, in a place where I knew very few people, seemed to magnify things.

On many days, I simply wanted to exchange a 5- or 10-minute neck and back massage with someone, or just wanted to cuddle for a few minutes after dinner. I had taken for granted how even brief exchanges of physical touch helped tremendously, such as a short neck rub in the car while I was driving, or an extended "good to see you" hug after a busy day. Now, I sometimes simply sat alone and cried. I also worried that my neediness would overwhelm my girlfriend.

Fortunately, because my new housemate and her partner were snuggle enthusiasts, things soon began to improve. Within a month or so, I was attending, co-facilitating, and sometimes creating snuggle events held in our home. I created and co-facilitated a snuggle for people in transition, and a few parties that blended snuggling with delicious foods like chocolate and waffles. I also co-created and co-facilitated a snuggle with a discussion about gender image.

As Stara and I got to know each other better, we started doing occasional massage and snuggle trades. Additionally, another friend began to invite me to smaller private snuggles, where there was great conversation, cuddling, and massage trading.

I Love my Cuddle Buddies!

All of this was incredibly helpful as I adjusted to various big changes in my life. It even benefited my new romantic relationship in a few ways. I wasn't quite as desperate for physical touch across the board, especially when I didn't see my girlfriend for a few days, or when we were having normal relationship growing pains. I was able to ease into things a bit more, as I knew I had a few other supports. The physical touch helped me to feel emotionally closer to my new friends, further increasing my sense that I wasn't overly dependent upon just one other person.

Also, exchanging massage often helped me to relax and get in a romantic mood more quickly, but giving lengthy massages had been a part of my girlfriend's day job for many years. She was understandably often too tired to exchange that type of touch with me at all. My getting some of these needs met elsewhere helped both of us.

Through the touch-positive events, I met many other people at the forefront or "cuddling edge" of the snuggle movement. This included individuals who have created a book and several cutting-edge workshops on healthy touch, another who writes about human relationship issues, and several members of the visionary group LoveTribe that was mentioned earlier. While some of these individuals began to develop snuggle party concepts years ago, the practice still remains largely unknown and mysterious to the general public. I'll share much of their wisdom with you in upcoming pages.

I learned a great deal by speaking with many of these deeply insightful and creative people, alongside attending and co-facilitating touch-positive events. The combination of snuggling, massage, conversation, and often delicious food left me feeling wonderfully energized and relaxed at the same time. Witnessing creations such as the new Tribal Love Network (a website for organizing snuggle parties and other touch-positive events) and participating in works such a brief internet video entitled *Touch* got me very excited about the possibilities. Attending touch-positive events with my new girlfriend gave me first-hand insight on how the event dynamics can impact couples—especially those still relatively new to snuggling.

Furthermore, I quickly became immersed in Portland's ecstatic dance community, which is also very cuddly in nature. Walking into the dance events, I had never seen so many people greeting each other with lengthy hugs, and often dancing with various partners in touch-positive ways. At other outings where many of these people were present, even musical performances and birthday parties, it wasn't unusual to see small groups of people happily snuggling. It was quite a shift from what I was accustomed to.

At the same time, the separation and divorce support group I regularly attended offered a stark contrast. There I often heard stories about how touch deprived people felt. When I described some of the touch-positive resources that existed locally, alongside concepts like snuggle parties, several faces often lit up. Someone would eagerly ask, "What's the name of the website where I can sign up?"

I came to realize that whether I was in a romantic relationship where many of my touch needs were being met, or between relationships, there were advantages to having a greater degree of physical touch with others. I had come to appreciate the importance of snuggle parties deeply, and knew I had to help spread the word to the broader public. Additionally, two years of foster parenting a young child had given me one more reason to help create a better world. If the next generation is to experience a more loving and connected world, the change needs to begin with us. Right now.

How might your life soon be much different, due to the power of snuggles? What new and energizing connections will you develop? When you look back in a few years, what will your own story of positive change look like?

3 Why Should You Be Throwing Snuggle Parties?

"Even though I'm a teacher, I sometimes have social anxiety. Well-facilitated snuggles have helped me to relax and connect without feeling the need to have a couple of drinks to loosen up. Also, becoming more touch positive has helped me come through times of stress, loss, or uncertainty with a more robust sense of resilience."

—M. M., age 43

Much research and observation tells us that nurturing touch enhances overall well-being, but it's easy to forget this in today's fast-paced world. Benefits of snuggling for human children and adults, as well as many other animals, include reduced stress, higher survival rates, lower blood pressure, improved immune response, and enhanced communication and memory. Some of these benefits also impact other aspects of physical and mental health.[4] How many of your current regular activities offer such a big bang for your buck?

At the moment we're born, contact with our mother produces a flood of chemicals that help to regulate our systems and enhance our physical and emotional development. The mother's body produces feel-good chemicals such as oxytocin in response to such contact, further reinforcing and encouraging her to bond with her infant. This helps to set the stage for connection throughout our lives.

In *Touching: The Human Significance of the Skin*, Ashley Montagu explains that "touch is the earliest sensory system to become functional in all species thus far studied, human, animal, and bird...the sense of touch, is the earliest to develop in the human embryo."

Early in the 20th century, the death rate for children below age one was virtually 100% in several US infant care institutions. The cause was often called *marasmus*, a Greek word meaning "wasting away." At that time, it was common for infants in these settings to receive little nurturing physical touch. As pediatric wards implemented simple "mothering" practices such as regular holding and cuddling of children, survival rates increased dramatically.[5]

As Kristen Reynolds points out on the "Nurturing Touch" pages of loving-community.com, simple physical contact such as gentle pats on the back and arms around shoulders is tremendously important. And men are not excluded; some research suggests that men need snuggling just as much, if not more than, women—they just don't always know how to ask for it.

For many people, physical touch may provide an especially important connection where verbal interaction alone cannot. In *A Cry Unheard: New Insights Into the Medical Consequences of Loneliness*, medical doctor James Lynch combines his own observations of heart data with a range of other research. Significant evidence suggests that interaction with other people provides a buffer against hypertension, heart disease, and other illnesses.

For many people, however, there's also an unfortunate flip side to social interaction: they experience significant stress while speaking to others, even when they appear calm on the surface. Such "communicative disease" is marked by significant elevations in blood pressure and heart rate, often even greater than what they would experience during moderate physical exercise. This is in contrast to being touched gently or listening calmly to another person without talking, which tend to lower blood pressure and heart rate.

Lynch believes that many of us learn to link stress with verbal interaction at a very early age, through observing adults' use of language in threatening or punishing ways, and through being silenced when we attempt to express ourselves.

Whatever the origins are, the effects of such repeated stress can accumulate to impact physical health over time. While Lynch describes ways we might make our verbal interactions more relaxed over time, in the shorter term we can also counteract both loneliness and stress in another way: with physical touch. It still requires some verbal communication, but not as much of it.

Research on some of our primate cousins underscores the importance of touch. In the "Harlow's Monkeys" experiment, baby monkeys were temporarily taken from their mothers and given the choice between a soft terry cloth and hard wire surrogate mother. They usually chose to cling to the cloth mother, even when they could obtain food only by clinging to the wire mother. This was likely because the soft mother more closely resembled their real mother—the similar touch was apparently even more important to them than food.

We know that even when another human isn't present, cuddling with pets can provide at least some of the same

benefits for people. Even more so, the benefits work both ways. Dogs left alone in a room, for example, show significant decreases in both heart rate and blood pressure—sometimes as much as 50%—when a human enters the room and then pets them.[6] Touch is a life-enhancing force for many animals.

In *Vitamin T: A Guide to Healthy Touch*, Bob Czimbal and Maggie Zadikov outline numerous types of nourishing touch, corresponding to a broad range of intimacy levels. Just a few examples include light tickling, playing with hair, kissing on the mouth, kissing on the cheek, cuddling, and massage.

However, many of us suffer from touch deprivation, largely because society teaches us that any type of touch might be misconstrued as sexual. So we often hesitate to touch each other at all. Many adults, including school teachers, are afraid to touch children. I recall a female high school teacher, probably in her fifties at the time, who was hesitant to touch students in any way because a female student had once accused her of sexual harassment. She explained that this was simply for putting her arm around the student's shoulder. The student may have had a history of abuse or trauma; but whatever the case, that interaction dramatically impacted how the teacher related to other students who may have welcomed—and potentially benefited from—such touch.

Additionally, many of us learn to withhold or reject both physical and emotional connection at the same times when we and our loved ones may need it the most. Some research suggests that children under three years old are already capable of practicing *relational aggression*.[7] This is the intentional withdrawal of affection or attention to punish someone else when we don't get what we want. We might learn this behavior from our parents, siblings, or peers.

When we carry these ideas of affection as a manipulative tool into adulthood, we can sabotage our ability to experience pleasure and intimacy, notes psychologist Stella Resnick in *The Pleasure Zone*.[8] For example, imagine that your partner forgets to get something at the grocery store, and because of that you act a bit less friendly and show less physical affection than you normally would that evening. Is that likely to get you a loving and affectionate response? Probably not. It might get you a half-heartfelt apology, and trigger further resentment. At the same time you're both already upset, you become unavailable to comfort one another.

Through learning that physical affection is so conditional and sometimes even manipulative, we may become more reserved about sharing it as freely. We may become wary of relying too much upon those closest to us for such affection, for fear that it may be withdrawn at any time. We may even come to feel that we don't deserve to receive physical affection from others at all unless we've first worked really hard to earn it. We no longer experience the full potential joy of any type of physical intimacy, because we're accustomed to it being a thing of scarcity, rather than abundance. Settings in which we can experience nourishing touch free of most conditionality, such as snuggle parties, can begin to reprogram some of this learning.

In the worst cases, individuals who don't receive enough physical affection can become aggressive and violent. Psychologist Alan Kazdin, who has spent decades researching treatments for children with severe behavioral issues, explains that when people don't receive adequate positive attention, they may attempt to get it through negative or undesirable behavior. Accordingly, his intervention strategies include simple actions like giving a child a high five when they're behaving well. Just a bit of positive physical contact is a starting point for putting an otherwise "doomed" child on the path to becoming a more loving adult.[9]

A few years ago, a young band billing themselves as a religious music group performed a rap song called "Christian Side Hug." They suggested that hugging a person of the other sex with the fronts of their bodies touching was overly sexual. To avoid the temptation of sinful premarital behavior, it was preferable to hug someone from the side. The group received much criticism from the general community, and also from Christians who did not want to be associated with them. Others called it out as a hoax, insisting that the group intended for it to be a joke. Whatever the intent, videos related to the performance garnered hundreds of thousands of views, and generated much discussion. Their performance struck a deep cultural chord: an all-too-common oversexualization of all physical touch, not limited to any particular religious affiliation.

What happens to children who are brought up in a culture with such mixed messages? They often turn into adults who dichotomize relationships when it comes to touch. Either they're platonically relating to another person, in which case they share little or no physical contact, or they're romantically involved with another person whom they expect to meet virtually all of their physical touch needs. They don't realize that there are many in-between options. As LoveTribe founder Jas Davis puts it, "There's a lot of terrain between a handshake and sex. We can all benefit from spending more time in those places."

This all-or-nothing approach can lead us to pursue physical intimacy in less-than-ideal ways. Consider the common approach of going to a bar or alcohol-serving dance club while lonely, hoping to "pick up" someone. We may believe that alcohol will give us the courage to say and do things we wouldn't feel comfortable doing in a completely sober state. But why would anyone even *want* to do things they're not comfortable doing when completely sober? Why look to substances like alcohol as a crutch for physical connection?

In some cases, we may be looking mainly for sex, but may not want to admit it due to the shame our culture often attaches to sex. Blaming our behavior on alcohol may feel easier than directly addressing our attitudes about sex. But in other cases, we may just want to get *any* type of physical and emotional intimacy in a relatively quick and easy way—but due to all-or-nothing thinking about physical intimacy, we believe that the only option is to be ready to go the whole nine yards with someone. But how can anyone feel comfortable having a full-on sexual connection with someone they barely know? Often, only with dulled judgment.

The irony, of course, is that if we do actually connect with someone under such conditions, our senses are also going to be dulled, and so we're not going to enjoy it as much. In fact, we may later experience more regret than joy. But if we can see that there are many "in between" possibilities, we can act in greater alignment with what we want, and we can meet our needs in ways that better respect ourselves and others. In many cases, going to a snuggle party might provide an easier way to get what we really want than going to a bar or dance club.

At times when you're comfortably in a relationship with a romantic partner, the all-or-nothing approach to physical affection may seem to work well for you. If your partner's various physical affection needs align closely with your own, you may indeed find that most of your needs are usually met through that connection. You may rarely need anyone else, and put little or no time into cultivating such connections. I admit that I still fall into this pattern quite easily.

However, life's curve balls can quickly expose the limitations of our usual social arrangements. For example, what happens if you lose a romantic partner through a breakup or death, they become ill for an extended period, or they become exceptionally busy due to career demands or other life shifts? You may suddenly experience much greater stress while your primary source of comfort is no longer available—at a time when you could use such comfort the most. As mentioned earlier, snuggles helped me tremendously during such a period.

And if something happened to you, wouldn't you take comfort in knowing that your romantic partner already had an existing support network to meet at least some of their physical affection needs?

We can all discover a greater wealth of nourishing physical touch, if we're willing to look slightly outside of the standard relationship boxes. Snuggle buddies and snuggle events can provide many social and emotional advantages over our usual ways of relating:

- Snuggle connections can feel **emotionally deeper and more nurturing** than the average friendship.

- While snuggle connections are not entirely immune from emotional dynamics like insecurity and tension, **such dynamics are likely to be less intense** than they are with romantic connections.

- For the above reasons, snuggle buddies and events provide a **quicker and usually simpler route to physical affection** than dating. You don't need to trust the other person enough to go out with them or to be sexually intimate. They just need to feel comfortable enough to snuggle with.

- Snuggles provide **opportunities to practice** saying "Yes" to what you really want and "No" to what you don't want. In a world that encourages passive aggressive communication, learning more effective approaches in a supportive setting can benefit other areas of our lives. This includes communicating with a current or future romantic partner about what you both want.

- If your only option for nourishing physical touch is romantic partnership, you can become caught in a painful catch-22 "desperation cycle" between relationships. The more desperate you become for touch, the clingier and less attractive you can become to potential mates. Snuggle buddies and snuggle events can **help to provide a buffer** against this trap.

The Date

- If you're between romantic partnerships, snuggling can **lessen the desire to make significant compromises** as you enter a new one, just because you're starved for any type of physical affection you can get. In your next relationship, you can be more confident that you *want* rather than desperately *need* your partner.

- Snuggle parties can provide opportunities to increase your touch comfort **at a pace that feels safer to you**. For example, perhaps you've always wanted to snuggle with several people at once, but fear that others might misinterpret your intent. At an organized snuggle event, participants' expectations are more likely to be on the same page, and support is more readily available. As one female snuggler explains, "Snuggles can be a marvelous way to indulge our needs for touch without as many social and sexual expectations. One can combine fun, pleasure, respect, and exploration with taking care of yourself."

- Snuggle parties **can relieve certain pressures on your existing or future romantic partner**, and vice-versa. Perhaps you desire exchanging certain types of touch that they don't. Maybe you love to trade foot massages, but your partner doesn't enjoy giving or receiving them. At a snuggle party, you may find someone else happy to do this.

- Through exchanging touch with a broader range of people, you're likely to **discover new ways you enjoy being touched**. This can help you to better enjoy other relationships, whether platonic or romantic.

- If you're currently in a romantic relationship, exchanging touch with other people at snuggles may help you to **better appreciate the unique ways in which your partner touches you**.

- The positive energy exchanged at such events can impact various parts of your being. When your own cup is overflowing, you'll likely have **more energy to share with others you love**, often in a variety of ways.

- If you're currently in a romantic relationship, and participate in snuggles with open and honest communication, they may give you and your partner an increased sense of freedom and decreased sense of total dependence that **enhances your mutual attraction**.[10]

- For some of the previous reasons, platonic snuggles might even **enhance your ability to meet sexual touch**

needs, enabling you to relate in a way that's more satisfying for you and your partner.

Snuggle parties have many benefits, and for some people could even prove to be viable alternatives or complements to certain medicine-based approaches. Granted, snuggling will never entirely replace the advanced skills of professionals such as massage therapists and acupuncturists. Nor are snuggle parties a replacement for mental health counseling for touch-based trauma—more on that later. However, snuggle buddy relationships, where two equal people are giving and receiving, offers different growth and connection opportunities than professional-client relationships, where each person generally has a very different and unequal role.

Being held and cuddled relieves my depression better than my drugs.

Reynolds 2013

As noted earlier, snuggle parties can provide a welcoming environment for touch that is not connected to sexual expectations. Having such settings is very important. At the same time, snuggle parties are not a total or permanent replacement for healthy and consensual sexual intimacy. For most of us, sex is a vital part of a fulfilling life; and I'm personally a big fan of sex. Snuggle parties simply focus upon a range of the physical touch spectrum that is different and also very important, but not necessarily superior. In a world where sexual touch is often unfairly demonized, it's important to be clear about this.[11]

That being said, increasing the accessibility of nurturing platonic touch is in some ways actually more radical than increasing the accessibility of sexual interaction. While this may seem counterintuitive, consider how many options exist for obtaining sex versus extended platonic touch like snuggling. The "world's oldest profession" is not professional cuddling, but prostitution. Add to that swingers' clubs, strip clubs, sex video chat websites, phone sex lines, matchmaking websites for sexual liaisons, and sexual want ads. Even if you're not currently in a relationship that includes sexual intimacy, it's easy to find sexual stimulation if you seek it.

If, on the other hand, you want to experience nourishing touch without sex, there aren't yet many options. If you don't presently have a healthy romantic relationship or high-touch family and friends, professional massage is one of the few related possibilities. A handful of organizations, social groups, venues, and solo entrepreneurs promoting snuggling-related services and events have cropped up globally.

However, until public understanding and acceptance increase, they may remain very limited in number.

Snuggle parties hosted by individuals like you, in living rooms and neighborhoods, can start to shift broader attitudes.[12] Through such interaction, our culture may eventually embrace the whole spectrum of touch in healthier ways.

4 Snuggle Party Ground Rules

"Snuggling taught me that touch is as infinite as color or music. Snuggling taught me that compassionate touch can be as powerful for emotional healing as talk therapy or antidepressants. Snuggling taught me that desire for sex and desire for touch are two different things."

—A. K., age 57

We cover ground rules in their own section, before any other logistical items, because they are absolutely essential. Even if you merely skim other sections of this guide before hosting your first event, please read this section all the way through.

An agreed-upon, clearly communicated set of ground rules is vital for creating a safe space for everyone. It is up to the group facilitator(s) to determine what actions to take if someone does not agree to follow them.

The rules that follow are adapted from Oregon Touch events and LoveTribe resources, with several modifications and additions. You can download a printable version at snuggleparty.org.

This relatively detailed list is not meant to be read in its entirety at every snuggle party. You might cover most or all of it once with newcomers, in an orientation event. You can give each of them a copy or let them know where they can access the full list on your group's website. Then you can do a brief review at each snuggle party, covering just the essence of each rule and leaving out the finer details. Just print out a copy and break out your fancy highlighter.

While the rules do not cover *all* possible situations, they cover most of the primary bases. The snuggle party definition provided earlier is included, as it's important for newcomers to be on the same page. As with other resources and suggestions in this book, you are free to modify the list to suit your own style and your group's needs.

List of Snuggle Party Ground Rules

Definition of a snuggle party:

A snuggle party is an event where participants share consensual, nurturing touch. Everyone is clothed, and the event is non-sexual. The energy is intended to be relaxing and soothing, rather than arousing or stimulating. Touch might include holding hands, exchanging back, shoulder, or foot massage, light facial touch, holding, playing with hair, or spooning. Open communication is emphasized. This includes stating one's own needs and boundaries, as well as asking for permission. More boisterous activities at snuggle parties can include playful wrestling, puppy piles (many people blissfully snuggled together), and pillow fights.[13]

- This is a **consensual** event. You are at choice at all times.

- **Ask for what you need**, and be comfortable saying "Yes" to what you need.

- You have the **right to say "No"** to any request or offer that you're even slightly uncomfortable with. No explanation is necessary; you may not be able to verbalize exactly why something doesn't feel right in the moment.

  - Even if you've already said "Yes," **you may discontinue** an interaction at any time if it becomes uncomfortable.

  - We use the "**sanctuary gesture**" (arms crossed over own chest with palms facing self, as shown in the following photo) to communicate non-verbally that we are presently closed to interaction.[14]

- If someone says "No" to you, verbally or with a sanctuary gesture, respect them and **respond graciously**. For example, "Thank you for communicating your boundaries openly and honestly."

- We use **leveling**, or adjusting each interaction to a level that both people are comfortable with. It's a way of getting to common ground and mutual respect.[15]

  - For example, if you ask if you can spoon someone, they may say, "No, but I would like it if you massaged my hand." You can then agree to massage their hand, propose another type of interaction, or thank them and politely decline to interact.

  - When offering to interact with someone else, wait for a response and remember that "No" always means "No."

- Don't assume that someone else is comfortable giving or receiving a certain kind of touch just because you are comfortable giving or receiving it.
- Don't assume that someone is comfortable sharing a certain type of touch with you just because they seem comfortable sharing it with another person.

- Sexually provocative clothing is **not recommended**. It's fine to have some skin exposed, and to be comfortable, e.g., standard shorts, short-sleeve shirts, and pajama-type bottoms are perfectly fine. However, a bikini top or a short, tight mini-skirt are probably not good ideas.

- **Touch in the "bikini area" is off-limits**, but try not to overreact if it seems to happen by honest accident.

- If joining two or more people already interacting, **ask permission** before joining in, and make sure it's okay with each of them. With a larger group, at least ask the permission of the person you'll be nearest.

- **Physical attraction**: From time to time, your body may show visible signs of arousal. This is normal, but you are responsible for not acting upon it in a sexual way, and for not prolonging potentially unwelcome contact. Simply shift your position and contact points, or get up and take a short break from snuggling. Also, snuggle parties shouldn't be an attractiveness competition, so consider snuggling with a variety of partners regardless of how physically attractive you find them.[16]

- Please **refrain from the use of substances** like alcohol that may impede judgment or ability to be fully present.

- **Confidentiality**: You may talk about your own experiences, and about the event at a general level, but you may not talk about anything that identifies a specific person or what they did. An exception is reporting ground rule violations to a facilitator. Because the general public does not yet understand snuggle events, some people may not want to be publicly identified as snugglers.

- **Privacy**: While snuggles are non-sexual, they're still relatively intimate, and we want a safe environment where everyone can relax. No videos, photos, or audio recording.

- **Personal hygiene**: Please avoid perfumes or other strongly scented products, as some people are sensitive to them. Make sure you've showered or bathed recently. Stay at home if you have a potentially contagious illness.

- **Conversation etiquette**: The rules of "normal" conversation settings become even more important in snuggle settings. Just as touch increases feelings of intimacy, it can also increase feelings of being violated when someone is breaking the rules. Imagine being at a party where you wish to go say hello to your friend across the room, but the person you're talking to ignores your hints and keeps talking. That feels a bit uncomfortable, no? Now imagine the same person is also holding your hand and stroking your arm, and not taking your hints. It feels even more like being held hostage, no?[17]

- Please **alert a facilitator** if someone is not honoring the ground rules.

Leveling: When I meet someone,

I might indicate that I would love to greet them with a hug.

But if they seem hesitant and offer a hand instead, I immediately level with a handshake.

Alongside the ground rules at snuggleparty.org that you can print, highlight, and take notes on, cuddleparty.com and meetup.com/oregontouch have abbreviated rules lists worth checking out. TribalLove.net offers this version:[18]

- Be present and consensual; ask permission and honor boundaries.
- Be aware of your boundaries and clearly communicate them.
- Keep your energy, play, and affection at a non-sexual level.
- Respect the confidentiality and privacy of others after the event.
- Please alert a facilitator if someone isn't honoring the rules.

If you choose to have new participants sign liability waivers, discussed later, you might include an overview of your ground rules on the same form. It can include language similar to the following: "The above ground rules were explained to me in an orientation session, where I had the opportunity to ask questions and gain clarity. I understand the rules, and agree to follow them to the best of my ability."

5   Becoming a Snuggle Magnet

"Attending snuggle parties over the past ten years has been hugely transformative in my life. The trust represented by entering a room with strangers, and then touching and talking with them on a deep, genuine human level, is profound in today's fear-saturated culture. I have made many wonderful friends at these events, and I have also enjoyed deep, nourishing connections with people I was never to see again."

—*M. S., age 41*

H opefully at some point while reading this book, you'll say to yourself, "I've got enough information, and now I'm ready to put a snuggle party on the calendar!" To make the event happen, you'll need to identify other people who are willing to try out snuggling—or at least try out activities that move them toward snuggling. And to do that, you'll need to be comfortable enough to invite people to engage in such activities. Here are a few suggestions for increasing your own comfort levels, getting a few other people involved, and establishing a presence.

Address the Past if Needed

This may or may not apply to you, but I include it at the beginning of the chapter because it's very important if it does. Some people seek out snuggle and cuddle events as a haven where they can once again receive and give safe touch, following touch-related traumatic experiences that have violated their boundaries. This might include, for example, rape or other forms of sexual abuse. Such trauma is unfortunately very common in our society, and is both a cause and a symptom of our culture's often dysfunctional relationship with touch.

Indeed, snuggle parties can be a valuable healing strategy in a comprehensive trauma recovery plan. However, this is only after one has already started work with a professional counselor or therapist. Snuggle parties are not a replacement for therapy.

In the case that you know or believe that you may have some type of touch-related trauma in your background, and you sense that could be hindering your ability to gain comfort with touch, I strongly recommend working with a counselor or therapist as you move forward. They can provide the depth of support that you need and deserve. Keep them posted on your snuggle-related plans, so that you can process things with them as needed. Otherwise, an otherwise potentially healing activity could trigger further trauma in you, and possibly even harm others.

Start with One-on-One Snuggling if You Want

For some people, inviting several people for a group snuggle event may feel easier than inviting someone to snuggle one-on-one. For others, it may feel easier to start with one-on-one practice before moving to a group. We're each in a different place due to our unique touch history, including presence or absence of touch traditions within our family, upbringing, and intimate relationship(s).[19]

Even if you have a strong desire to start snuggling as soon as possible, breaking the ice and softening the boundaries to establish a snuggle buddy can feel awkward. I still often feel awkward approaching someone and asking them to snuggle, even in an organized group setting. It takes practice, so be self-forgiving while gently stretching your boundaries.

If you prefer one-on-one practice before hosting a group event, start by asking a friend you're already pretty comfortable with. Encourage them to read the first few chapters of this book. Consider a platonic "date" where you practice snuggling together, perhaps during an activity like watching a non-romantic movie or favorite television show.

If no friends fit the bill, ask your friends for other people they're comfortable recommending. Remind them that you're not looking for a potential romantic partner—just someone you feel safe and comfortable snuggling with. If your existing connections don't yield any leads, you might check some of the sites listed in the "Additional Resources" chapter to find a potential snuggle buddy.

If none of the above approaches are fruitful, there are always more generic personal ad sites. There, it's especially important to explain what snuggling is, possibly even providing some informational links to sites such as snuggleparty.org. Be explicit that you're not seeking a sexual or romantic partner, but don't assume this will automatically rule out individuals who may get the wrong idea. Hopefully as cuddling and snuggling grow in popularity, language and understanding around this will improve.

In any case where you don't already know someone, especially if a friend can't vouch for them, having a one-on-one snuggle session may raise personal safety concerns. While there's no replacement for your own judgment and discernment, following are a few suggestions. Use, modify, or discard at your discretion:

- Ask any potential snuggle partner to meet in a public place initially, just to talk and learn more about each other. This could be a coffee shop, community center, or restaurant. Don't share your home address, and insist on each person paying for their own food or beverage to avoid any dynamics of obligation.

- Make it clear that there won't be any snuggling on the first meeting, and that it will likely take you a day or two to get back to them. This way, you won't feel pressured to give a "Yes or "No" on the spot, and you'll have an easier out if you don't resonate with them.

- If you're getting a pretty good vibe on the first meeting, ask permission to hug before saying goodbye. While you want to allow a bit of leeway for awkwardness, any discomfort you feel during a hug will likely be magnified during snuggling. Trust your instincts. If needed, meet a few new people to gain practice and perspective before making any decisions.

- Should you get the sense that you're doing something to make the people you meet uncomfortable, ask for honest feedback in an email follow up, with an explicit promise not to shoot the messenger. But don't take it personally if you don't get a reply at all.

- Have your first snuggle date in a relatively public space with furniture or pillows, such as a library, community center lounge, or church parlor. If the weather is nice, meet in a relaxing but non-secluded area of a park and bring a picnic blanket.[20]

- Let a friend know the details of your first snuggle date, along with your snuggle date's identity. Ask your friend to expect an "I'm okay" call or text from you afterwards. Let your snuggle date know that you need to leave by a given time because a friend is expecting to hear from you.

- Schedule your first snuggle date or two during the daytime to lessen the likelihood of it feeling romantic.

Recruit and Invite Other Snugglers

There are several ways to approach this, depending on factors such as how much you wish to meet and snuggle with totally new people, and whether you prefer to facilitate small or large events.

Begin with games Instead of Snuggling

If you're not getting any takers for snuggling, see whether a few friends or acquaintances might be up for a party that includes touch-positive games. The "Connective Games and Activities" chapter includes a range of fun possibilities. At the end of the event, include a conversation or brainstorming session about future events that might include snuggling. Some people are more receptive to possibilities after experiencing the connection and energy of a few touch-positive games.

Start Small: Invite Only People You Know

If you believe some of your friends may be interested in snuggles, invite just a few of them via phone or email, or invite only close connections through a non-public social media event page. It's up to you whether invitees can bring additional guests.

Some friends might be skeptical simply because they don't have a clear idea of what a snuggle is. Once they know, they could be totally into it. Expect to receive some questions. If you don't get the desired response on the first try, consider having a Q&A social event where you simply talk about snuggles, and answer questions people might have.

Make it clear that there won't actually be any snuggling at this event, and that your intention is simply to gauge interest in the types of events people would be interested in. It could be a potluck, or it could be a meet-in-greet where you simply provide beverages or light snacks. You might include a few touch-positive games with only moderate levels of touching, emphasizing that any participation is optional.

Private invitation events have several upsides. You have more control over who attends. You're more likely to be comfortable snuggling with many of the guests, and there's like to be less unpredictability around what guests' needs may be. Even if invitees can bring additional guests, you know that they're already approved as not-too-weird-or-crazy by someone you trust. Also, some guests may be more comfortable attending an event that's not publicly visible on a social networking site, out of fear that work colleagues, relatives, neighbors, or others may judge them.

However, relatively private events have downsides as well. You won't meet as many new and different people, some of whom could be amazing connections. Also, just because guests are all connections of yours, doesn't necessarily mean they will have snuggle chemistry with each other. Allowing each invitee to bring an additional guest they're comfortable with can help to address these issues.

Identify Those Likely to Need Touch the Most

You might also consider what types of people may be the most in need of touch. A few examples are people who have recently ended long-term romantic relationships, those who have lost a romantic partner to death, those who have recently located from another geographic location, or those who wish to rebuild or expand their social support network for whatever reason. Perhaps you have a friend or loved one in a long-term residential care or health facility, and want to bring an occasional snuggle party to them. If you happen to fit one or more of these categories, your events may present an opportunity to help others while also helping yourself.

Blend Snuggling with Other Fun Activities or Themes

Another way to build a snuggling community is to create events that blend touch-positivity with activities that will appeal to other interest groups. Then see if the facilitator(s) of that group would be willing to share information about your event. Or, share it yourself if you belong to the group and you're relatively certain that doing so doesn't violate their spamming policies.

For example, because I'm mostly plant-based and have written waffle and chocolate cookbooks, I created and co-facilitated a chocolate snuggle and a vegan waffle / snuggle party. I advertised the events among a few food-related groups.

Other fun examples:

- If you're also interested in hiking, create an event that includes a hike, picnic snuggle, and shoulder massage trade. Everyone brings their own blanket to snuggle on.

- If you're new to a town, create a snuggle specifically for people new to that town. Shortly after arriving in Portland, I created and co-facilitated a snuggle for people facing major life transitions.

- If you really enjoy massage, create a snuggle where participants are also encouraged to trade massage. If you enjoy some type of massage in particular, such as foot massage, why not host an event that encourages just that?

- If there's a particular movie you've been wanting to see, and would love having people to discuss it with, create a movie viewing snuggle.[21]

- If you love the outdoors, host an outdoor snuggle, and invite people from a group that hosts outdoor and nature-based events. Ask to use a friend's yard if you don't have ample space.

- If you want to see a live performance, organize an indoor or outdoor Cuddle Concert.[22]

Cross-promotion with other groups may be especially beneficial for snuggle parties because many people are still not familiar with the concept. This is even more the case if you're relying upon online communication. Some social networking websites ask users to enter a list of interests, and then they use this list to automatically recommend relevant local groups, events, and activities to their users. "Snuggling" and "cuddling" are not yet activities that most people are likely to add to their personal interest list. Therefore, alongside categorizing your group under more popular interest labels, connecting with existing groups is very important.

Because most people still do not understand the concept of a snuggle party, they may occasionally react in unpredictable ways to your advertisements. This happened to me once, when the facilitator of an online food interest group threatened to ban me if I ever posted a "snuggle" again. This was even though my snuggle included a potluck that meshed perfectly with their specific food niche. After kindly explaining the concept of a snuggle and requesting clarification as to what rule(s) I violated, I never received a response. But at least I wasn't banned. So proceed at your own risk, don't be discouraged, and try not to take any misunderstandings personally.

Encourage Word of Mouth

One of the easiest ways to spread awareness is through word of mouth. People often do this naturally, but it never hurts to provide encouragement. Ask participants to tell their friends about events they've enjoyed, both in person and via online social media networks. If you have one or more web pages established for your group, ask people to share it. If you know a few people who seem to be very popular and have a lot of friends, ask them personally if they'd be willing to attend your event, and to invite their friends as well.

Post Group Info and FAQs Online

If you're throwing events that are open to a large and relatively public group of people, consider using a social networking site or other web page to minimize the time you spend answering frequently asked questions. Here are a few pieces of information you'll likely want to include in easy-to-find locations:

- What is a snuggle?

- What are the basic ground rules?

- When and where are upcoming event(s)?

- How much, if anything, do the events cost?

- What are the annual financial and time/participation investments, if any, expected of members?

- Who facilitates the events, and what relevant background or credentials do they have?

- Whom do I contact if I have questions or concerns about any event?

- What are the mission and vision of the group?

- In what ways can I get involved, for example, by hosting, facilitating, or volunteering? How do I get involved?

A few of these items, such as the definition of a snuggle and ground rules, can be adapted from sections of this book or from snuggleparty.org. FAQ's on snuggle events are also on sites including CuddleParty.com and TribalLove.net.

As for where to post your group's page, a few social networking sites, including one devoted to touch-positive and heart-centered events, are listed in the "Additional Resources" chapter. Because these sites are still growing, some geographic areas already have a significant number of members, while others currently have very few. As they continue to gain members over time, they'll become increasingly useful—not just for group events, but for people seeking individual snuggle buddies who meet certain criteria, such as positive recommendations from existing friends.

Synergize with Existing Groups

Earlier we explored the idea of incorporating other types of activities into your snuggles, and considering other groups whose members may also benefit from your events. Through cross-promotion, each group can reach more people. For example, your city may already have one or more groups hosting sexual events, but there may not yet be many offerings for non-sexual touch-positive events. Some people in the existing groups may crave additional touch of a non-sexual nature. Likewise, some people who join your group first may eventually wish to explore a more sexual group as well. Your groups may help to build one another's membership.

Before starting your group, do a bit of research on popular social networking and event sites to see what groups already exist in your area. In some cases, it might make sense to join forces with an existing group. In other cases, if your personality and style seems very different from that of another facilitator, it might still make sense to start your own group even if a somewhat similar one already exists. They won't necessarily compete with each other, as different personalities and styles appeal to different audiences.

Portland, Oregon, for example, once had just a few ecstatic dance events each week, and now it has well over a dozen. However, few of them seem to truly compete with one another. I've been to ecstatic dances hosted by at least a dozen different facilitators, and each has had a unique feel. And if it hadn't been for a few of the larger and more broadly advertised dances that introduced me to the practice, I may have never checked out some of the smaller events. Similarly, it's difficult to imagine there being too many snuggle parties. The world desperately needs more snuggling!

6 Obtaining and Caring for Fluff

"Snuggles have had an enriching effect on my life. Growing up in middle class America, it was taboo to touch people. I recall even having this fear of brushing up against my friends or strangers. But, as I opened myself up to different cultural modes of thought, I explored such things as snuggles, and found that touching and being touched in a controlled environment is quite liberating and much needed!"

—*G. B., age 40*

The term *fluff* refers to the soft items attendees sit or lie on while they snuggle. It's one of the most important elements of the physical setting, so we cover it in its own chapter here. In the next chapter we'll cover a number of other ideas for creating a cozy setting.

You really don't need much to get started, especially if you're just having a handful of friends over to begin with. The couch and a futon pad or inflatable mattress may be plenty. But should you decide you need more equipment to create a comfortable setting, you'll find useful information here. Sometimes it's fun to get fancy!

Some of the items below can be expensive if purchased new. Consider thrift stores, garage sales, Craigslist, and Freecycle if you wish to keep your initial financial investment low. Also, many stores will put items such as seasonal sheets and blankets on sale or clearance near the end of their season.

Fellow snuggling enthusiasts might also have items to donate. Once you have enough people interested, consider asking several to pitch in to purchase a few gym mats, air mattresses, or other items for collective use. Ask friends and relatives if they have items they'd be willing to contribute.

Snuggle Padding

If you already have a relatively soft carpeted floor and a few pieces of comfortable furniture, you may not need much more padding to begin with. You can always start small, and then add items with other people's help as attendance grows. The very first snuggle I attended was in a carpeted living room with a couch, loveseat, and several plush velour blankets on the floor. There were plenty of pillows, but no additional mattresses or pads. However, the floor did become a bit uncomfortable after a while, so I eventually sat up against a couch.

While sheets will hide any minor stains on used underlying padding like futon pads, be aware that older padding can present issues with mildew and dust mites if not cared for properly.

Even if you have a very soft and well-padded carpet floor, you'll probably still want to put some type of covering over it, as carpets and their underlying padding can still hold a lot of dirt and allergens, even when they're clean on the surface. And even a padded carpet that initially feels comfortable to lie on may not feel the same with the added weight of someone's arm or leg draped over you—as can often happen at snuggle events.

Following is a comparison of several types of snuggle padding, with pros and cons for each. Given the broad range of products available, I'm unable to recommend or endorse specific brands or models within any category.

Couch or Love Seat

Pros: If you already have one or both of these items, and they're set up in the room where you plan to host events, it makes sense to use them. Couches and love seats are great for people who want some physical contact, but who find that snuggling while lying down feels a bit too intimate for them.

Cons: The number of people and snuggle postures they can accommodate are limited. It may be difficult for people to lie side by side on either.

Futon Pads

Pros: These can often be folded for more compact storage or for moving from room to room, and you don't need to inflate them. They're more comfortable and breathable than inflatable options. If the frame is already located in the room where you plan to have your events, then folding it out to create additional space may take minimal effort. You can also use the pad without the frame.

Cons: Although lighter than a regular mattress, futon pads can still be somewhat heavy and awkward to move. If stored rather than used regularly, they take up more space than inflatable mattresses.

Thick Inflatable Mattresses

Pros: These are lightweight and portable, and they occupy minimal storage space. They are available at a range of prices, thicknesses, and quality levels, and can be used for indoor or outdoor snuggles.

Cons: They can take time to inflate and deflate, although this time is greatly decreased if the mattress is paired with an electric pump. They can develop leaks, and can sag a bit when several people are piled on. Because they're not breathable, they can become slightly uncomfortable on a hot day; but this is less noticeable with sheets or other coverings.

Foldable Gymnastics Pads

Pros: These are available at a range of prices and quality levels. Many are lightweight, easy to store and transport, and relatively compact. Some but not all have a covering that makes them moisture proof and suitable for both indoor and outdoor snuggles. They don't take time and effort to inflate. They can be laid out together to form a large snuggle surface, especially if they have connective Velcro edging. They can be stacked two high if some attendees find them too thin.

As a snuggle community forms, you might ask attendees to purchase their own foldable pad to bring to snuggles.[23] Consider asking that they all fall within a given thickness range so they form a roughly level snuggle surface when laid out together. I've personally found pads between one and two inches thick to work fine.

Cons: A whole set of decent quality pads can be expensive for one person to buy, so a group investment effort may make most sense. However, because snuggling causes far less wear and tear than doing gymnastics, you probably don't need the most durable pads available. Thinner pads may require doubling for some people. Moisture-proof surfaces may feel sticky in warm weather, but this can be minimized by using sheets and keeping the room relatively cool.

Thin Camping Sleeping Pads (foam or inflatable)

Pros: These are lightweight and easy to store and transport. They are also available at a range of prices and quality levels. Each person can easily bring their own, in cases where you may not have enough padding to accommodate everyone. If they're inflatable, they're generally quicker to inflate and deflate than thicker inflatable mattresses.

Cons: These are likely to hold only one or two people each. With multiple pads of differing thicknesses, it can be difficult to create a contiguous and level snuggle surface for multiple people.

Standard Bed-Quality Mattress

Pros: It's difficult to beat the comfort of a full-fledged mattress for snuggling. Most people already have one, and it can be used to add extra snuggle space.

Cons: Hosting a snuggle event in your bedroom might feel a bit too intimate or send an ambiguous message. Moving a heavy and bulky mattress to and from another room will likely require assistance, and you'll need to re-make your bed afterwards.

"Cuddle Mattress" Bed-Quality Mattress

Pros: This specific brand of mattress is made partially of foam slats, forming slots to accommodate arms and toes. This allows snugglers to remain in certain positions more comfortably for longer periods—e.g., one person can have their arm underneath and around another person without it falling asleep. According to its creator, Mehdi Mojtabavi, it is also useful for individuals with certain physical and medical conditions.[24]

Cons: You may need help moving the mattress from room to room if you sleep on it and want to have snuggle parties in a separate room. Many individuals would find it very expensive to buy just to snuggle on. However, it may seem a wise investment to those who also plan to sleep on it, to organizations or groups who plan to use it for snuggling frequently, or to those who have difficulty snuggling comfortably on other furniture due to physical conditions.

Caring for and Storing Padding

Consider whether you want to allow food and drink on or near padding, as spills can be difficult to clean. Also be careful about storing padding like futon mattresses in basements or other places prone to humidity, so mildew doesn't develop.

If you join others to purchase communal fluff, and plan to use it at different locations, purchase items that are durable enough to withstand the wear and tear of being loaded and unloaded for transport and storage.

Sheets and Blankets

Sheets are a great idea as they help to keep the underlying fluff clean, and they will make any surfaces that aren't as breathable (e.g., inflatable mattresses and gymnastics pads) much more comfortable and cozy. They can also make a room look cozier as a whole. A sheet on a couch or love seat can help it to blend in with other sheet-covered fluff, giving it all a warmer and more bedroom-like feel.

While it's not critical to wash sheets after every event unless food stains, massage oil, or the like are a concern, doing laundry every few events can still add up over time. If that's not something you're willing to do, ask others to help out by bringing sheets. If you want to be extra considerate of your guests, consider laundering all your fluff coverings in non-scented or minimally scented detergents, as some individuals are very sensitive to perfumes.

Although they can help to create an even cozier feel, blankets aren't absolutely necessary unless you're expecting cooler weather. It's generally good to have a few on hand in case people need them, but you can also ask people to bring their own if they tend to get cold easily. Soft blankets can also take the place of pillows if you have a pillow shortage.

Pillows and Pillowcases

You likely already have a few of these on hand. They don't all need to be full-sized bed pillows; even smaller pillows such as those used on couches and chairs can help. While nice pillowcases can give older pillows new life, keep in mind that heavily used pillows more than a few years old—especially if used without pillowcases—may be a haven for dust mites and a trigger for allergies. Consider asking people to bring their own pillows, alongside providing only a few of your own. This will also save you the time and effort of washing additional pillowcases.

Massage Equipment

The padding you use for snuggling will generally be sufficient for occasional massage trades. That being said, if you're serious about having frequent massage at your events, you might consider obtaining a massage table. It can provide a more comfortable position for both the giver and receiver.

New massage tables can be spendy, but used tables are sometimes available for a fraction of the cost. Try to find one that folds and has carrying handles, if you wish to transport it to events in different locations.

Another option is to find someone who is willing to bring a massage table to events, either as a kind favor or perhaps in exchange for not having to pay an admission fee. Someone who has been doing massage as a job for a long time may not be excited about attending such an event, but someone who is still building their practice might be seeking opportunities to showcase their skills.

An important related note: Any massage trades at an event advertised as a snuggle party should follow the same touch guidelines outlined in the ground rules for snuggle parties. If massages are going beyond those boundaries—for example, if you're allowing people the option of stripping down to their underwear for oil massages—the additional types of touch allowed should be clearly stated in the event announcement. Even if it's still not sexual, it is more intimate touch, and everyone attending should be clearly informed as to what to expect. This is addressed in more detail later, in the section "Always Let Guests Know What to Expect."

7 Creating a Comfortable Physical Setting

"Snuggling has made it possible for me to go much longer without a boyfriend, so that I can be more choiceful in my romantic relationships."

—*K. R., age 51*

A

lthough fluff is one of the few essential ingredients needed for a basic snuggle, taking the time to create an even cozier environment can make a really great snuggle. While your own creativity and intuition are the best resources, below are some suggestions to get you started.

Hanging Tapestries

These can be very helpful in larger spaces, either to cover a wall to make the room feel cozier, or to create a smaller feeling area within the larger room. One snuggle I attended was in a gym, where the facilitators hung a few wall tapestries from a rope across the middle of the room to partition off a smaller snuggle area. They also covered the mats with sheets and blankets and strung up dark blue holiday lights. These small changes transformed the space significantly.

Lighting

The main rule of thumb here is to avoid lighting that is too bright. Dimmer lighting generally produces a cozier feel. If you have really bright overhead lights in the room where you plan to host your events, consider purchasing a smaller lamp or two with tinted shades, or with bulbs advertised as giving off "soft" light. Then turn off the overhead lights. If you're using low-wattage bulbs that don't get very hot, such as LED bulbs, you can use a thin colored scarf to create a makeshift shade or light filter.[25] Just make sure the scarf is a safe enough distance from the bulb to avoid any type of fire risk.

A small string or two of single-color holiday lights, especially those in darker shades such as blue, green, or red, can also provide a decorative soft glow for a low cost. Candles are also great, if they can be placed in spots with little risk of being knocked over. Keep in mind that people can lose track of where their arms and legs are while shifting around on snuggle fluff, and may be disoriented briefly when getting up to walk to the bathroom, grab a snack, or get a drink.

Of course, you can also adjust lighting toward the "less cozy" direction if needed. Should you have difficulty getting guests to leave after a gentle hint or two because they're so comfortable cuddling, turning brighter lights back on can help to return people to a more alert state.

If you're hosting an outdoor snuggle in the early or late evening, tiki torches, a fire bowl, or mosquito-repelling candles can add warmth. A string or two of miniature lights hung from a tree, shrubs, or fence can also create a relaxed ambience.

Music and Sound

In my opinion, music with few or no vocals is best, as it is less distracting. Also, it shouldn't be very loud. I've facilitated and attended a few events where background music played through a cell phone was plenty loud. Live acoustic guitar music, played softly, also creates a wonderful atmosphere.

Try to set things up so that you can just press "play" and largely forget about it, or so that you don't have to participate in the performance yourself. You may want to get in some quality snuggle time yourself amidst tending to other hosting responsibilities, so you probably don't want the additional responsibility of having to assist with the music.

If you have instruments traditionally used for mindfulness and meditation practices, such as a singing bowl, chime, or bell, these can be useful for setting the tone (no pun intended) at the beginning and end of the event. Invite participants to close their eyes and take several deep breaths while listening to the tone, and reflect upon what they wish to experience (or did experience) at the event. I've even been to a few events where a didgeridoo player provided participants with a "didg bath" of low frequency sound to get them in a more relaxed and present state. Trust your creativity.

Heating and Cooling

If a lot of people are in a relatively small room, they'll warm it up significantly, especially while snuggling. So if your event is in the summer time, be sure to have a fan or two on hand if you don't have air conditioning. Sweat and snuggling are generally not a winning combination.

If your event is during cooler months, keep in mind that guests will be able to feel drafts especially well while lying on or near the floor. This is even more the case if the snuggle is in the same room as the door where guests are entering and exiting. If this is the case, it's probably best to clearly communicate both "doors open" and "doors closed" times for the event, as discussed under "Managing Logistics Smoothly." Extra blankets are always good to have on hand; and small radiant heaters or space heaters can be useful, if they can be set up in a safe manner in a relatively crowded room.

If your space has a wood or gas fireplace, and the room is large enough to operate it safely alongside a floor full of snugglers, then you can create a wonderfully cozy atmosphere in cooler weather. In cases where room size or attendance may make it difficult to have a full-fledged fire safely, or where maintaining such a fire would be too much hassle, a single commercial long-burning fire log can provide a bit of soft light and warmth. Even something as simple as placing several candles in a fireplace can enhance the feel of a space.[26]

If you're hosting an outdoor snuggle during nice weather, consider a shady location to lessen concerns about overheating and sunburn. Snuggling in the sun can feel nice if the temperature is relatively cool, but at the very least make sure there's an easy place to retreat for a break in the shade if needed.

Food and Beverage

Having some food and refreshments at a snuggle can make it more welcoming. After a few hours of snuggling, getting all that oxytocin and other feel-good chemicals flowing can give you the munchies! Also, when engaging in activities like trading massage, keeping the body hydrated is important for muscle relaxation.

However, food and extravagant beverage are not required for a snuggle. I've been to a few that offered nothing more than water, and still had a great time. If you want to add a bit of class but still keep it very simple and inexpensive, put water in a nice pitcher with a few lemon wedges. For more variety during cool weather, heat up a pot of water shortly before guests arrive and put out a few teas. During warm weather, make a pot of tea and chill it in the refrigerator. Herbal or decaf teas are a good bet because caffeine can make it harder to relax while snuggling, and some people are sensitive to caffeine. Where possible, leave beverages unsweetened and allow guests to add their own if they wish.

If you want to have food, and also want to minimize your shopping and food preparation time and costs, have a potluck-style event where attendees bring snacks. Or keep the food and beverages to a minimum by making sure the events fall shortly after a standard meal time. Dessert themes are one way to have some food but still minimize overall time and financial expense.

Consider encouraging snacks that are both healthy and rejuvenating, such as fruits, vegetables, nuts, and some sweets. Items that are vegan, gluten-free, and low in added sugar will cater to a broader range of guests. As suggested under the ground rules, alcohol-free events will encourage participants to remain fully present.[27]

You might ask guests to keep food and beverages in an area away from the snuggle, with some exceptions like water bottles with closing tops. Because people often lose track of where their arms and legs are while snuggling, and can feel a bit disoriented upon getting up, it's easy to knock things over. A spill can quickly put a snuggle surface out of commission for a while. Also, most people will be walking around in socks or barefoot, and probably don't want to get salty peanuts or pretzels stuck between their toes. Crunch! Ouch!

Scent Sense

Our sense of smell can have a very profound effect on our mood. Scented candles, incense, smudge sticks, potpourri, and essential oils can help to create a relaxing environment.

However, keep in mind that some individuals are sensitive to strong scents, so consider subtler approaches such as a small scented candle or two.

If your kitchen is near your snuggle space, even putting a bit of water in a saucepan with a few dashes of your favorite spices, and allowing it to boil for several minutes, can create a wonderful but not overbearing smell. If you want to use something stronger like incense or a smudge stick, consider using it half an hour before the event, allowing time for the scent to dissipate.

Because guests will be snuggled up in close proximity to each other, you may wish to have a general ground rule that they refrain from applying any strong scents to themselves, such as perfume or cologne, within a few hours of the event. In such settings, one over-perfumed person can create olfactory mayhem and sneezified snuggles for a dozen people. As suggested in the ground rules, remind participants to be mindful of body odor, and consider washing the day of the event. Some people consider showering or bathing just a few times a week healthier for the skin, but not everyone may be comfortable with this practice when in close proximity.

Wet Shoes and Coats

If there's any chance of rain the day of your event, make sure that guests don't have to cross over any snuggle surfaces while walking between the entrance and the shoe and coat pile. Nobody wants to snuggle on a damp surface. Also try to keep dry any places they'll be walking after they've taken their shoes off, such as the route between the snuggle area and the bathroom.

Cleanup

Cleaning up can take considerable time, especially if you're feeling very relaxed after snuggling. Tasks may include removing sheets from fluff and laundering them, deflating air mattresses if necessary, putting away mattresses or pads and pillows, moving back any furniture you temporarily removed from the snuggle space, and washing dishes and cups. If any attendees volunteer for cleanup, you can either ask them in advance to stay for a specific amount of time after the event ends, or ask them to complete specific tasks before leaving.

Ideas if Space is Limited

Perhaps you really want to facilitate events, but live in a very small apartment, have roommates or housemates who just aren't open to the idea, or have too much "stuff" occupying your home. Following are a few possible alternatives. Some may also be useful if you live in an area that's inconvenient for people to travel to.

First, check with friends to see if one of them would be willing to host. If you're having difficulty finding volunteers, consider offering a portion of any admission fee as rent. Sometimes people with the most beautiful spaces welcome a bit of assistance in paying for them. At the same time, some snugglers appreciate the value of comfortable settings, and are willing to pay a bit for them. I recently attended a snuggle event in the small but beautiful living room of an apartment with large windows, looking out onto a beautifully green courtyard full of trees. While the event itself was quite simple, the setting alone was well worth the small contribution requested. We had an enjoyable three hours, and the host thanked everyone for helping her with that month's rent—a win-win situation!

If you or a friend has yard space, consider an outdoor snuggle during a time of the year when the weather is likely to be nice. A public park can also provide a great snuggle party setting. Depending upon where you live, be cognizant of factors such as mosquitoes. I attended a really cozy outdoor evening snuggle where tiki torches with citronella helped to keep the bugs at bay.

Explore businesses that may have padding already available, such as gyms or martial arts studios. They may allow you to use the space for a reduced cost, or perhaps initially for free, if you're using it at a time when it's not otherwise in use.

A business such as a café might have a private meeting room or other space available for rent, or possibly for free if you require each guest to purchase some food or beverage. Of course, you'll still need to provide the fluff. Small dance studios, wellness centers, and yoga studios are other possibilities. An art studio could make an aesthetically interesting setting for a snuggle.[28]

Some public spaces such as libraries and community centers have meeting rooms available. They will likely have guidelines regarding events; for example, any event held there may need to be open to the general public. Check the websites of local organizations such as the public library and department of parks and recreation to see what facilities are available in your neighborhood.

8   Managing Logistics Smoothly

"Snuggling deepens my platonic bonds while enriching all my relationships and adding an overall ease of communication. It builds a stronger, more authentic connection between my community and myself."

—*E. G., age 37*

O nce the fluff and other physical setting pieces are in place, the remainder of the safe and comfortable snuggle setting depends largely upon your facilitation. Clearly communicating ground rules, as discussed earlier, is a key part of this. Considering the suggestions below can make the event even more relaxing and fun for attendees, and more rewarding for yourself.

Keep It as Simple as Possible

As an event host, you likely have some interest in snuggling yourself. However, this won't happen if you're busy with host-related responsibilities the entire time. You may wish to keep your first few events as logistically simple as possible.

Follow some of the suggestions for simplifying in the "Creating a Comfortable Physical Setting" chapter. This includes keeping food and beverage minimal, so you don't have to worry about things like replenishing the salsa bowl or putting out more ice. Let people know in advance that they can bring a snack, but that the primary focus is snuggling. If you want music, set it up so you can press "play" and forget about it, or find a volunteer who enjoys music to manage it.

Also, determine what home preparations you'll need to make to host the number of guests you want to accommodate. If it starts to feel like too much effort, consider a smaller snuggle party. You can always facilitate larger events as you gain experience.

Manage Energy around Last-Minute Responders

You'll often receive a few last-minute calls or messages from people who want to know directions, want to know if they can bring an additional person, and so on. As a host, you'll want to do your best to answer your guests' questions. However, don't expend too much energy on "last-minuters" if you're already feeling rushed to create a good-as-possible space for everyone else.

You'll have to decide your own policy regarding whether and how you respond to last-minute inquiries. Do your best to anticipate and answer any questions in the invitation materials. I sometimes ignore messages within the last hour or two before an event, unless it's something really important, something that won't take more than a minute or two of my time, or something that I failed to include in the invitation materials.

Opening Circle

Because snuggles are very interactive in nature, it's best if everyone starts out on the same page, and also has an opportunity to warm up to each other if they haven't already met. This is where an opening circle can be helpful. You can have participants literally sit in a circle, perhaps even holding hands, or just remain seated wherever they happen to be.

During this time, you'll want to introduce yourself, describe the locations of amenities including bathroom, water, and food (if applicable), remind participants of any key time points (e.g., "'We'll be starting cleanup around 9:30 and ending by 10:00"), and cover ground rules. You'll also want to give everyone a chance to introduce themselves. Along with their name, you might ask them to share what they enjoy most about snuggling, or something good that happened to them that day. You might simply give them the option to share whatever is at the forefront for them, whether it happens to be positive or negative. This way, they can get some emotional support at the snuggle if needed.

You can announce some type of per-person time limit for introductions, e.g., one to two minutes, so that participants don't feel they're being cheated out of snuggle time. Some facilitators simply have participants go in order clockwise or counterclockwise. Others use a stuffed animal, small ornamental pillow, or other object that can be passed or tossed from one person to the next, with the person holding it being the only one allowed to be speak. This visual aid can reduce the likelihood of people interrupting one another. It's natural for people to be excited to see each other at the beginning of an event, and to want to talk and catch up.

Snuggle facilitator Kristen Reynolds often asks people to describe whether they feel more like a puppy or a kitten as they introduce themselves to the group. (You can also use *dog* and *cat* if you prefer.) You may find these definitions helpful to share at your parties:

You're a puppy if you're feeling relatively open to a range of touch. Once you've given somebody permission to touch you, they don't need to ask beforehand each time they want to touch you in a different place or way, as long as they're within the general ground rules. It's fine for them to try something different and then ask how it is for you. You'll let them know if something isn't working for you.

You're a kitten if you don't like surprises, or are feeling more specific about how you'd like to be touched. Even if you've already given someone permission to touch you, they should ask before touching you in a different place or in a different way.

If you're not sure whether you're a puppy or a kitten, it's best to say you're a kitten.

Doors Open and Doors Closed Times

Because snuggles are very interactive in nature, they don't often lend themselves well to a "show up whenever you'd like" approach. Consider having a "doors open" time when people may start to arrive at your event, followed by a "doors closed" time at which the door is literally closed to new arrivals. Advertise both times clearly in your invitation. Shortly after the door is closed, begin your opening circle where you share introductions, communicate ground rules, and so on.

Such an approach avoids several potential pitfalls. I share these as someone who has been in the shoes of the facilitator, the on-time participant, and the late participant:

- Any time new people enter a room, it impacts the energy a bit. If they're still feeling a bit of anxious energy from their trip there, this will impact people who are already relaxed.
- If someone is in the middle of introducing themselves and sharing where they're at, someone entering will distract others from listening to them.

- A person entering late may have missed important things that others have shared about themselves. For example, what if one participant shares that they have a very tender sprained ankle and don't want anyone putting any pressure on it?

- A person entering late may miss the review of the ground rules. This increases the odds that they may neglect to follow some of the rules, and it also may make other participants feel less safe.

Plan Boundaries and Support in Advance

Setting healthy boundaries for yourself, as well as determining what support you need to make the party happen, is important to do ahead of time. The questions in the following ideasheet are designed to help you clarify what you want. Your answers don't need to be lengthy or perfect, but spending some time on them will increase your odds of having an enjoyable party. You can also download a printable version of this sheet and other resources at snuggleparty.org.

Snuggle Party Visioning Ideasheet #2

What aspects of planning and hosting a snuggle party are you the most excited about?

What aspects of planning and hosting a snuggle party are you the least excited about?

What conditions or limits do you need to put in place to make your snuggle party as awesome as possible—not just for your guests, but for you?

Examples: minimum and maximum number of guests, the time by which you want guests to leave, the maximum amount of money you're comfortable spending.

What supports do you need to put into place to make your snuggle party as awesome as possible—not just for your guests, but also for you?

Examples: Recruiting a volunteer to help with the aspects you're least excited about, finding a babysitter.

Create a Setup Checklist

It takes some time to get fluff set up for a snuggle, especially if you need to move any furniture into or out of the room, clean up the room, or inflate any air mattresses. You may also need to do some food and drink prep, print out your attendance list, locate your printed list of ground rules to review during opening circle, and so on.

If anyone has volunteered to help out, and your checklist seems overwhelming, consider asking them to come a full hour early. If you end up being ready ahead of schedule, you can always enjoy socializing.

Following is a checklist that you can use as-is or modify as needed. You can also download a printable version at snuggleparty.org.

Snuggle Party Preparation Checklist

Your party may require more or fewer items than what appears on this list.

Invitation and Event Description

___ Prerequisites for guests if any (e.g., having attended an orientation)

___ What to bring (e.g., own pillow, food if potluck)

___ Location and transportation/parking directions

___ Attendance cap or other attendance restrictions (e.g., sex balancing, whether invitees can bring guests)

___ Start and end times (including doors open/closed times if desired)

___ RSVP deadline

___ How to pay, if contributions requested

___ Link to ground rules

___ Reminder about policies like no strong scents or alcohol

Physical Environment

___ Padding to snuggle on

___ Pillows

___ Covering for fluff

___ Heating or cooling (fans/AC, or heat/blankets)

___ Music

___ Lighting (may include candles)

___ Wall hangings and other "cozy" decor

___ Signs (e.g., "please leave shoes at door")

Food

___ Snacks

___ Beverages

___ Plates and utensils

___ Napkins

___ Serving bowls

___ Table space for food and beverages

Logistical Items

___ Nametags and writing utensils

___ Printout(s) of ground rules

___Waivers for guests to sign

___ Jar for contributions

___ Attendance list

Additional Items

___ Item #1: _____

___ Item #2: _____

___ Item #3: _____

9 Connective Games and Activities

"No matter how many times you say 'You like me' or 'You love me,' if you never touch me, there's some part of me that never believes you...If you had a lover and they never touched you but only said they love you, you'd have a hard time believing that they even loved you. It's the touch that drives that message. It's the touch that you believe. Someone who says 'I love you,' and they're giving you a hug, they're holding you, they're caressing you, *that* feels like love."

—K. R., age 51

ometimes we need to be eased into snuggling, through increasing levels of intimacy and connection. That's where connective games and activities come in.

As open-minded as I consider myself to be, I did not become comfortable with snuggling overnight. I heard about it several years before I actually developed the courage to try it. Even after a number of snuggles, I still feel pretty shy and awkward on occasion. Each of us has a different set of life experiences, upbringings, and cultural values to which we've been exposed. These all impact how long it takes us to become comfortable with snuggling.

Healthy touch expert Bob Czimbal likens the touch level of snuggling to that of slow dancing—the differences being that snuggling has much less movement, is not synchronized to music, and is often done lying down instead of standing up.[29] Most of us have slow danced at some point, perhaps sometimes even with people we didn't know that well. We may have been shy about it at first, perhaps dancing on our own amidst the crowd before we had the courage to slow dance with someone. Chances are, we've often found it warming and soothing once we finally had the courage to do it. It's very familiar to most of us, and probably feels moderately intimate.

However, if we remove music, movement, and standing upright from slow dancing, there are few distractions from the sensation of the physical touch itself. That can make it feel even more vulnerable and intimate. Consider how many people would be willing to caress each other and rock back and forth without music, for a period of 5 or 10 minutes. Now imagine them caressing without rocking at all, and while lying horizontally instead of standing up. Does this make it easier to see why many of us may initially be shy about snuggling? This is possible even if the actual amount of touch isn't far beyond what we have already experienced in other settings.

Fortunately, there are ways to help people get closer to the same page when it comes to snuggling, and at least become comfortable enough with themselves and others to begin exploring. The slow dance versus snuggle analogy above provides some clues.

It can be helpful to start with activities that involve interaction but minimal touch. Trust and rapport take a bit of time to build, as people are feeling each other out. Other stimuli such as movement and sound can lessen the intensity, by providing a bit of distraction and dissipating some of the energy—much as music does with dance. At the same time, movement encourages people to drop out of their heads and relax into their bodies. The first set of activities in this chapter falls into this introductory category.

Following initial introductions and icebreakers, you might move into activities that educate participants about important snuggle-related concepts. This includes basic knowledge and skills around boundary setting, leveling, and ground rules. This foundation increases the odds that they and others will have a positive experience as they move into touch-based interactions. Alongside presentation of information such as ground rules, you might demonstrate concepts such as leveling with another facilitator, and encourage participants to practice by interacting with one another. You might also facilitate discussion. The second set of activities in this chapter falls into this arena.

Once participants have a basic foundation, you can engage them in a few touch activities less intense than snuggling. This allows everyone to ease into snuggling, rather than feeling like they're being forced to zoom from 0 to 60. The third set of activities in this chapter falls into this category.

There's no hard and fast rule regarding which activities to include in an orientation event. Following is just one agenda possibility. While a snuggle at the end can provide a practice opportunity, excluding one from orientation-specific events can simplify logistics and leave more time for other topics. If you include a snuggle, emphasize that it's optional.[30]

Example orientation agenda:

- outline of event agenda and facilitator introduction

- participant introductions

- one or two icebreaker games, with minimal levels of touch

- discussion and educational activities covering important concepts like ground rules, leveling, cultural differences, and distinctions between sensual and sexual touch

- two or three games that incorporate touch, with increasing duration and level of physical contact

- optional snuggle, with facilitator(s) readily available

In LoveGuild's event planner training, conscious touch expert Shanya Luther offers an agenda strategy for easing new snugglers into increased connection. Between other exercises, invite participants to roam (described later). Each time, ask them to stop at a random point and pick a new person near them as a partner for the next exercise. End your pre-snuggle activities with an exercise involving groups rather than dyads. "Touch Angel" breakout pods, described later, are one great example. Then ask groups to combine to form larger groups. From this point of connection, invite them to transition into snuggling. This structure also encourages participants to gain experience with more people, and to see that a monogamy model doesn't need to govern nurturing platonic touch.[31]

The activities vary in level of intensity, and it's important to remind attendees that they are always at choice. They don't have to participate in any activity that feels uncomfortable, and they may discontinue an activity at any time. A given exercise may trigger strong emotions, either positive or negative, for some people; and two participants may have completely different experiences with the same activity.

Amy Baker of Envision Arts Studio authored a number of games for the following sections, as indicated by her name below the titles. She's adapted some of them from the improvisation communities with which she's been involved. If you'd like to experience more of Amy's inspiring work, check out her site at envisionplay.com. Other games are gleaned largely from various events I've attended, incorporating some of my own variations, interpretations, and combinations.[32]

In general, these activities are suitable for groups of at least six people, and no more than fifteen. If a specific game has a different ideal size, it is mentioned in the description. When there are uneven numbers for pairs, one of the leaders might jump in, or there can be a group of three. It can be difficult to simultaneously facilitate and participate, so it is ideal to have two or more leaders.

Interactive Games with Minimal Touch

The activities in this section are useful for getting people familiar with one another, and encouraging them to drop into their bodies, through interacting with minimal physical contact. Consider using one or more of these activities as ice breakers near the beginning of an event. To raise self awareness, ask participants to take note of how they experience themselves and others at this level of interaction. What curiosities do they have? What reactions do they notice within their body and mind? With whom are they eager to interact more? What reservations do they have?

The Name Game

Adapted by Amy Baker

You might introduce this name game to the group as "Human Tape Recorder" or "Copy Paste."

Have the group stand in a circle. After explaining the game, the leader begins by turning to the person immediately to the right, and says their name to that person, along with some type of vocal intonation, facial expression, and/or creative body gesture. For example, they might say "George!" in a growl while lifting their arms like an orchestra conductor and standing on tiptoe. Intonation and physical gestures are included to help participants drop into their bodies and become more comfortable with one another.

The second person then turns to the right, and repeats the name and movement to the third person, mimicking the intonation, expression, and gesture to the best of their ability.

Each person copies what was passed to them as closely as possible, but they might inadvertently add something new as well. For example, they may pause, chuckle, and sigh before turning to the next person.

The third person then turns to their right, mimicking what the second person did. They include the new material added by the person they just observed: the pause, chuckle and sigh.

This continues until the first name has been passed all the way around the circle and back to its owner. Then the originator says his or her name one more time.

Then the next person to the right creates an expression and gesture to go with their own name, and starts this going around the circle. For example, she may say "Mary" with a lilting tone and a smile, while hopping on one foot. Play continues until each person's name has traveled around the circle.

Remind participants that they are copying what was just passed to them, not what the original person whose name is being passed did. After everyone has had a turn, you might quickly go around the circle in the opposite order, having each person repeat his or her own name and gesture, just to reinforce learning each other's names.

Synchronized Group Breathing

While this involves minimal physical contact, it helps participants to become more attuned to others' bodies, alongside their own. Conscious breathing also aids in relaxation.[33]

Ask everyone in the group to sit or stand in a large circle, or to break out into smaller circles, optionally holding hands or placing their arms on the backs or shoulders of those on either side. Lead them through the following variations:

- Deep breath in, hold for three to five seconds, followed by slow, deep exhale. Repeat three times in unison.
- Deep breath in, hold for three to five seconds, followed by an "om" or other sound on the exhale. Repeat three times in unison.
- Fast, shallow breaths for 10 seconds, panting like a dog; doesn't need to be in unison. Invite participants to bounce up and down slightly, flexing at their knees. They should stop immediately if they start to feel lightheaded.

Going into Business Intros

By Amy Baker

Have people get into pairs, and instruct them to share with their partners about a hobby or interest, such as wine tasting, fishing, painting, or tango. Ask them to choose a hobby as different from their partner's hobby as possible. Just take one to two minutes for each person.

After everyone has shared with their partner about a hobby, introduce the next part: ask each pair to come up with an idea for a business that combines the two hobbies. Don't tell them about this part until they've shared their hobbies with their partners.

Then have the group come back together as a circle, with partners standing together. Each pair introduces themselves to the group, saying their names and the business idea they have created.

"Anyone Else?"

This game allows participants to share some personal details about themselves if they wish, to discover things they have in common with other group members, and to experience a bit of touch positivity.[34]

Participants start by standing in a circle. One at a time, they volunteer to stand in the center and state a personal characteristic or past experience they'd like to share with the group, followed by the phrase, "Anyone else?" For example, the volunteer may state, "I enjoy eating anything that contains chocolate. Anyone else?"

Anyone else for whom the volunteer's statement is true—in this case, anyone who loves chocolate—then walks to the center of the circle and joins hands with others standing there. Before returning to the outside circle, those in the center take a few seconds to look around and acknowledge others standing with them.

After the participants in the center return to the outer circle, another volunteer goes to the center and makes an "Anyone else?" statement. They might say, "I've attended a U2 concert. Anyone else?" Others who have seen this band perform live would then venture out into the center.

Play continues until everyone in the group has volunteered at least once.

My Favorite Things

By Amy Baker

This is a creative variation of "Anyone Else?" that allows for more nuanced opinions and expression.[35]

Have the group stand in a circle. The leader asks people to step into the center as far as they agree with the statement made. For example, if the statement is "I like chocolate," a person who loves chocolate would move into the center of the circle, while someone who dislikes chocolate would remain at the edge, with people placing themselves anywhere in between according to their feelings about chocolate. The leader offers several examples, then invites people to make statements related to their touch preferences.

Examples:

I like shoulder rubs.

I don't like being having my feet tickled.

I'm shy about approaching others to snuggle until I get to know them.

I prefer to be asked before being touched.

I grew up in a family that shared lots of healthy touch.

At the end of the game, take a few minutes to debrief. Ask how it was for people, what they noticed, and so on.

Roaming, with or without Music and Dancing

Invite participants to stand up and slowly mill about the room for several minutes, exchanging a few seconds of eye contact and gentle non-verbal acknowledgment with each person they pass. This can be a soft smile or even just a slight head nod—whatever feels most authentic for them.[36]

For a bit of variation, ask participants to switch their demeanor at a few points during the interaction. For example, invite everyone to look at each other with welcoming gazes during the first minute or so, with curiosity the second minute, and then perhaps with playful flirtatiousness the third minute. Remind participants that they're free to opt out of interacting at any time.

Some other possible variations:

- Invite people to touch hands or even just fingers as they pass each other.

- Invite participants to behave like their favorite animal, greeting others with their animal voice as they roam around the room. Other possibilities include their favorite element (earth, water, fire, air), vegetable, or even household appliance. Use your imagination!

- Put on a playful song and invite participants to dance around the room. They're free, but not required, to make physical contact with others. However, they should at least make eye contact. Encourage them to continue to roam around, interacting with a range of people.

Elbow Dance

By Amy Baker

This is another fun variation on the roaming exercise. Put on some music and ask participants to greet each other nonverbally using their elbows. How many ways can you interact with someone elbow to elbow? Then suggest interacting one at a time with other parts of the body: pinkies, shoulders, and feet.

Guided Meditation and Progressive Relaxation

Inspired by Sally Dubats

This exercise builds upon a few tried-and-true techniques from the counseling and group facilitation worlds. It can take from 10 to 20 minutes, depending upon how deep you wish to go with it. It's designed to get participants relaxed and dropped into their bodies before interacting.

If you have a meditation chime or singing bowl, you can use it at the beginning and end of the exercise, but this is not necessary. Also, soft background music can add to the mood.

Have participants lie down or sit up in a relaxed and comfortable position. They can hold hands if they wish, but should otherwise be in their own space. In a slow, gentle voice, guide participants through the following dialogue. Feel free to modify as you see fit; many variations are possible.

Close your eyes, or find a spot on the ceiling to relax your focus in a soft gaze—whatever is most comfortable for you.

We're all going to take three slow, deep breaths in unison. With each inhale, take in relaxation and nourishment. With each exhale, release anything in the way of being fully present in this moment.

[Take three slow, deep breaths in unison.]

After the third exhale: *Spend a few moments feeling the nourishment of your breath coursing throughout your body.*

After a short pause, choose one of the following options:

Option #1: *Imagine the most relaxing place possible. It might be someplace you've actually been, or someplace you dream of being. It might even be a place on another planet. Allow your imagination to run free.*

Or:

Option #2: If you enjoy being creative, describe a scene in detail, such as a beach on a tropical island, a bed of pine needles in a forest next to a waterfall, a soft clearing in a beautiful wildflower garden, or even a pillow of clouds floating beneath the sunshine. You might even take them on a trek through the clouds to a distant planet. Go through each of the senses vividly, e.g., describing the feel of warm sunshine trickling down each arm, or the playfulness of a soft breeze over skin.

After a minute or two of setting the stage with one of the options above...

Ask participants to tense and then relax different muscles, from head to toe, as they're in their imaginary environment.

You don't need to cover every muscle, just some of the places where people commonly hold tension.

For example:

As you lie in this relaxing space, feel gentle energy enter your jaw. Tense your jaw for a moment to hold the energy. [Pause.] Now let it totally relax, allowing the energy to flow away, carrying away any tension, and leaving just a gentle warmth. This part of your body is now at peace.

Now feel the energy enter your shoulders. Tense them by raising them up toward your ears. [Pause.] Now drop them and let them totally relax...

Now feel the soothing energy enter your hands. Clench your fists for a moment to take in the energy...

Repeat the tense-and-release instructions for a few other body parts, such as abdomen, buttocks, calves, feet, and toes.

Finally, close the exercise gently: *We're now going to return to our present surroundings, bringing with us the relaxation and warmth we've generated. We're again going to take three slow, deep breaths in unison...*

Following the breaths: *Take a few moments to regain your bearings, and as you're ready, open your eyes.*

Educational Activities on Important Concepts

While you'll need to cover some basic information about snuggles in a lecture or discussion format, simply talking to an audience for an hour or more isn't the optimal way to share knowledge. Especially when the topic involves touch. The activities in this section provide foundational information to help participants move into touch-based activities safely and enjoyably. Active participation will enhance their learning, increase familiarity and bonding, and make things much more fun!

Simple Shoulder Touch

By Kristen Reynolds

This activity illustrates how even very simple touch can trigger a more relaxed state.

Ask participants to get into pairs, with one person volunteering to be the initial receiver, and the other one the initial giver. The receiver should sit in a comfortable position with their arms at their side, and hands resting on the floor or in their lap. The giver should stand or kneel behind the receiver, facing the same direction. The giver's shoulders should be at least a foot above those of the receiver.

Before other participants proceed, you might wish to demonstrate the following with a volunteer.

Instruct the givers to place both hands on the shoulders of the receiver, and to press down gently for about 30 seconds.

They shouldn't use much muscle strength at all, but simply lean forward so that some of their weight is supported by the receiver's shoulders. The receiver's job is simply to receive the touch. Receivers are free to ask for more pressure if that would feel good, or to say "Lighter" or "Stop" if it feels like too much. Givers are also free to discontinue at any point.

Ask participants to observe any internal or external physical reactions they witness during the interaction. Then, they should shift roles with their partners and repeat the exercise. Afterwards, invite everyone to share what type of physical reactions they noticed.

Common reactions include a deep sigh or exhale, slowed breathing, and a relaxation of the shoulder and neck muscles. You can explain that the more relaxed state is partially due to the release of touch chemicals like oxytocin. In the case that one or more participants have neutral or negative reactions to the touch, invite them to consider what that means about their touch preferences. They may or may not choose to share their insights with the group.

Leveling: Demonstration and Role Plays

While leveling is covered briefly in the suggested ground rules, it's good to include at least one activity around this concept because it's so important in touch-based interaction.

There are many cases where two people are interested in sharing touch, but person A requests a type of touch that feels too intimate for person B. Rather than simply saying "No," B may suggest a modification that they're comfortable with. A may agree to B's alternative, or may suggest yet another option to which B can respond "Yes" or "No." Negotiating to a common denominator that both people are comfortable with, as a way of establishing mutual respect, is called leveling.[37]

Example:

Person A: *Would you mind if I spoon you?*

Person B: *That feels a bit too intimate for me, so no. But I'd love it if you'd gently run your fingers through my hair while sitting next to me. Would you be willing to do that?*

Person A: *I'd be happy to do that for a few minutes, if you'd be willing to do the same to me afterwards. How does that sound?*

Person B: *That sounds awesome!*

Because leveling is more complex than yes/no interactions, it's probably best to begin by modeling an example or two with another facilitator or participant who is already familiar with the concept. Then you can have participants practice leveling in the following way:

Have participants break up into pairs, and pick a personal characteristic that can easily be used to designate a "person A" in each dyad, e.g., the shortest person, or person with the birthday closest to January 1. Again, if there is an odd number of people, the facilitator may pair up with someone.

Instruct participants to complete the following tasks with their partner:

- Person A makes an initial physical touch request. The initial request should be relatively simple and brief, such as "May I hold your hand?" or "May I massage your shoulders for a few seconds?" Person B politely declines the initial request, but offers a modification or alternative that they're comfortable with. Person A then has the option of accepting or suggesting another alternative. They continue negotiating until they've agreed, at which point they engage in the touch interaction.

- The people in each pair switch roles: Now person B makes the initial request, and person A declines and offers a modification or alternative. The rest continues as above.

- Ask participants to find another partner, preferably someone they don't already know, and repeat the exercise.

Yes/no Role Playing: Dyads

This gives participants the opportunity to practice the following: saying "Yes" to what they want, saying "No" to what they don't want, asking for what they want, and learning to respect and graciously accept "No." Additionally, it can build each person's confidence that they can trust their own "Yes," as well as the "Yes" of someone else.

It's best if each person has the opportunity to interact with a few other people, because their comfort levels may vary with different types of people. Differences in sex, age, race, perceived sexual orientation, and body type can all impact someone's comfort level in negotiating touch.

Ask participants to pair up with someone else in the room, preferably someone they don't know well. If there's an odd number of people, you or another facilitator may pair up with someone. Announce some trait that can be used to easily designate a person A and B in each dyad, e.g., the person with the longest hair is "A."

Instruct each pair to do the following:

- Person A makes at least three different physical touch requests of their partner, one at at time. They should be simple and brief, such as "May I hold your hand?" or "May I massage your shoulders for a few seconds?"

- When responding, Person B should try to include at least one "Yes" and one "No." They reserve the right to say "No" to all requests if they're not comfortable with any of them. Following each "Yes," the pair actually engages in the physical touch for several seconds.

- A and B now switch roles, with person B now being the requester. Each pair repeats the steps above.

- Ask each person to find a new partner, again preferably someone they don't know very well. Announce another trait to designate Person A and B, e.g., the oldest person is "A," and instruct the new pairs to repeat the steps above.

After the exercise, ask a few people to share what their experiences of saying and hearing "No" and "Yes" were like, and what communication strategies seemed to work best.

Jas Davis adds this advice for coaching people to say and hear "No" more effectively:

Reply to a "No" with "Thank you for taking care of yourself." This is affirming for both people as the person replying stays in an empowered and positive position. They are proactively honoring the power of the other, expressing their support and care. It also reinforces that the reply is not personal to the asker so much as to the respondent.

A "No" is actually a gift because the respondent's capacity to say "No" makes it possible for the asker to ask for what they want (because the asker can trust the other person to take care of themselves). Knowing the responder can say "No" means we can trust their "Yes," too. We also encourage respondents to say "No" without saying anything else, to reinforce that there's no need to give a reason or excuse.

Yes/No Role Playing: Groups

By Amy Baker

This variation of Yes/No Role Playing with groups helps to reinforce the importance of a) asking permission before joining a group of two or more snugglers, and b) consulting with other members of one's group if necessary before granting permission for such a request.

Have roughly two-thirds of the participants break up into groups of two to four people. Instruct the remaining participants to roam around, asking for permission to join groups, being as persuasive as possible. Groups should say "No" to the first three of four requests from roamers, providing whatever reasons they wish, before finally saying "Yes."

After the groups start to say "Yes" and all roamers have joined groups, ask a few participants to share what their experiences of saying or hearing "No" and "Yes" were like.

Hug/Handshake/Zen Bow

By Amy Baker

This is an icebreaker for people to greet each other near the start of an event. It also offers another opportunity to practice the important concept of leveling. Another way to describe leveling is the practice of always staying  at the touch level that you have in common with another person. For example, if John wants a level of 5, which might mean spooning, and Sue wants a level of 2, which might mean holding hands, they have level 2 in common, so they stay at that level.

This exercise also helps people to develop or continue a practice of checking in with themselves about comfort with different levels of touch, and what feels right to them in the moment. The Zen bow involves just eye contact, the handshake has some physical contact but at a level that is more familiar and equivalent to a business setting, and the hug, of course, has the highest level of contact of the three.

Participants mill around the space, then approach another person. As a pair, they decide together—preferably without speaking—which of the three options they will do together. If one person puts her arms out in a hug gesture, and the other person puts one hand out to shake hands, the pair will do the handshake, since this is a lower level of touch than the hug.

When you discuss this exercise afterwards, ask if anyone felt that the bow was in some way more connective or intimate than the other choices, since it involves eye contact.

Re-leveling Demonstration

As one female facilitator reminded me, one of the more difficult times to say "No" is after we initially agree to allow another person to snuggle with us, and later find ourselves uncomfortable with some way in which that person is touching is. This may be due to a new type of touch for which they didn't gain consent, or a continuation of a type of touch we initially agreed to but no longer want.

Unfortunately, some people may fear they are being too picky or prudish by asking a person to refrain from a certain type of touch. Instead of simply requesting an adjustment in the moment, or *re-leveling*, they may instead refrain from interacting with that person in the future, or even from attending any more snuggle events.[38]

This type of situation is not covered in simple yes/no/leveling exercises. One way to teach participants about handling this type of situation is to act out a snuggling scenario with another facilitator, where one of you models a polite request for a behavioral shift.

Several key pieces are helpful to model in a re-leveling demonstration:

• Use "I" statements rather than "you" statements to describe your wants. This sounds less blaming, and is less likely to make the other person feel attacked.

- Begin the request in a positive way by noting something you like, so that the person is more receptive to the second part of your statement where you're requesting a change.

- Use *and* rather than *but*. It's easy for a listener to discount everything before a *but* as something you really didn't mean, and intend to cancel out with whatever follows.

- Alongside explaining what you *don't* want, explain what you *do* want: offer a replacement behavior that is acceptable to you.

- The person receiving the request should respond graciously and appreciatively, and should wait for a reply if they offer another alternative.

Example 1:

Person A: *I enjoy snuggling with you, and I don't want a hand so close to my breast. Would you like to put your hand on my shoulder instead?*

Person B: *Sure. Thanks for letting me know!*

Example 2:

Person A: *I like how you've been touching my neck lightly, just how I asked, and now it feels like I've had plenty. Would you mind just resting your hand on my neck?*

Person B: *I appreciate the heads up. Actually, my arm's getting tired in this position anyway. Can I rest my hand on your stomach?*

Person A: *Yes, that sounds nice.*

Participants can then chime in with additional ideas regarding how they might phrase such a request. Remind everyone that they still have the right to end an interaction altogether, at any time, for any reason. Re-leveling is just one option if they're feeling uncomfortable at a given moment.

Facilitated Discussion on Snuggly Topics

This type of activity allows participants to become more familiar with each other, and with important touch-related concepts, at a slower pace and in a less physically intimate way.[39] You might facilitate discussion on specific topics as a part of an orientation event, or you might facilitate a discussion as part of a snuggle party.

Some possibilities:

- Discussion about a movie or video on a touch-positive topic. This could be a short online video like *Touch*, listed in the additional resources section. If participants wish, they can snuggle during the movie.

- Discussion about personal touch preferences. Instruct participants to break out into small groups or pairs. Ask them to talk with each other about how they do and don't enjoy being touched. This will inspire thinking about the types of touch they may wish to say "Yes" and "No" to, and will allow them to practice clarifying and expressing preferences.

- Discussion about one or more specific cultural barriers to snuggling, massage, or other touch. You might have an all-male discussion around homophobia and male touch, an all-female discussion around setting comfortable touch boundaries with men, or a discussion about meeting touch needs for people in a specific age range.

- Discussion around a book chapter on a touch-positive topic, such as those found in *Vitamin T: A Guide to Healthy Touch*, listed in the resources section. An Oregon Touch event included a segment where participants shared their personal touch histories. You can discuss cultural influences, attitudes about touch learned from families of origin, and so on.

Interactive Games with Touch

These games are intended to be played after participants have been introduced to one another, and preferably after they've covered basic ground rules and concepts like communicating yes/no boundaries and leveling.

Roughly speaking, the earlier games in this section tend to involve less intimate touch while those later in the section are likely to feel more intimate to participants. An exception is the Angel Wash, which is listed near the end because it works well as a closing activity. I say "roughly speaking" because everyone is different, and what feels less intimate to one person may feel more intimate to another. Also, some of the earlier activities offer less opportunity to talk explicitly about touch before engaging in it, so they may actually feel like a more rapid stretch than some of the later activities. I encourage you to experiment with the many options available here, and to see what resonates best with you and your participants.

Remind everyone that they are free to modify or halt an interaction at any point, if they begin to feel uncomfortable for any reason. Encourage use of the sanctuary gesture, illustrated earlier under "Snuggle Party Ground Rules," and again later under "Options for Addressing the Sensitive Stuff."

I'm a Tree

Description by Amy Baker

Participants stand in a circle. One person begins by stepping into the center and saying, while raising their arms like branches, "I'm a tree." Then a second person steps in and adds anything that goes with a tree, like a park bench, squirrel, acorn, or leaf. They might act out the thing they named, or not. A third person adds another element. Bonus points for adding something that interacts with or touches the others in the center in some way. Get playful!

After three people have formed a scene in the center, the tree chooses one of the other two to step back out with them and become part of the circle again.

The remaining person starts a new scene by repeating what they are: "I'm a squirrel." Then two more join in: "I'm a..." and "I'm a..."

After three people have formed a new scene, the squirrel chooses one of the other two to step back out with them and become part of the circle again.

Each time, the person who started the scene chooses one of the other two to step out with them, and the remaining person carries their character over into a new scene.

Play continues until the facilitator senses that people have had almost enough of it—better to go too short than too long. If you can find an appropriate moment to bring it back to "I'm a tree," it makes for a graceful ending point.

Example:

Person 1: *I am a tree* (steps to center, arms out as branches).

Person 2: *I am a leaf on the tree* (holds Person 1's arm).

Person 3: *I am the grass under the tree* (lies down and curls up around Person 1's feet).

Person 1: *I'll take the grass* (1 and 3 step out, rejoin circle).

Person 2: *I am a leaf.*

Person 4: *I am a sun ray shining on the leaf* (massages leaf's shoulders).

Person 5: *I am a cloud* (playfully comes between sun ray and leaf).

Person 2: *I'll take the sun ray* (Person 2 and 4 rejoin circle).

Person 5: *I'm a cloud.*

Person 6: *I'm a rainbow.*

Person 3: *I'm a pot of gold.*

Person 5: *I'll take the rainbow* (5 and 6 step out).

Person 3: *I'm a pot of gold.*

And so on...

Human Sculptures One

By Amy Baker

This game needs a minimum of 6 people, and is best played with no more than 15. Have your group stand in a circle. After explaining the game, the leader begins by stepping into the center and striking a pose. Two other people join in, creating poses that physically connect with the first person and interact with the initial pose in some way.

For example, the first person steps to the center and covers their eyes, then the second might stand shoulder to shoulder beside them and cover their ears, and the third joins in by touching shoulders so that they are all in a row, and covers their mouth. Then someone titles it, "See no evil." The three people step out, and the titler steps in and strikes a new pose. Titles can be humorous, poetic, playful, serious, or creative in any way.

Anyone who is not part of the sculpture can think up a title for it. The facilitator repeats the title to the group. Generally choose the first title spoken. If two are said at the same time, choose the one that feels like it fits best, or let the group decide. The person who named the sculpture then steps into the center to begin the next sculpture, and the three who were in the center rejoin the circle.

Play continues for about 8 to 10 minutes, or whenever the facilitator feels the group has had a chance to fully experience the game but is not yet bored.

Human Sculptures Two

By Amy Baker

This game is best played with at least 10 or 12 people, the maximum being 20 or so. Have people get into groups of three or four. Each group chooses someone to be apple, another person to be banana, and a third person to be orange. If there is a fourth member, they could be mango.

Apples go first as sculptors. Give the group a word, such as *isolation, harmony, vulnerability*, or *connection*, or come up with your own. Choose words that describe different states of interpersonal relating. Sculptors place their human clay into poses in relation to one another that evoke or describe the word they have been given. For example, if the word is *isolation*, the sculptor might place people with their backs to each other, looking down, arms crossed, not touching.

After participants have had a few moments to experience the pose, give the group another word, with bananas playing the role as sculptors. Continue for 5 or 10 minutes, or until each person has had a few opportunities to be a sculptor.

Human Knot Game

Description by Amy Baker

This game works well with a group of at least five people. If there are more than 10 people, split the group into two circles, with each circle playing separately.

Everyone reaches into the center with their right hand and takes the hand of someone across the circle. Then all do the same with left hands. Each person holds hands with two different people. The trick is to figure out as a group how to undo the knot without anyone letting go. Discussion is important—mention that listening to each other and cooperating is a big part of the game. At the end, some people will face out and others will face in. Give a group cheer when you get the group untied!

Masters and Minions of Love

By Amy Baker, adapted from Matt Weinstein

Have participants form groups of three. Each group chooses one person to be the Big Kahuna, the Main Cheese (or "Top Tofu" if you prefer a diary-free option), and the Top Dog. Big Kahuna goes first as master. They tell the other two, who are acting as minions of love, how to spread love around the room. This may include giving hugs or shoulder rubs, telling people how beautiful they are or that they are loved, saying specific appreciations to each person, and so on.

The person who is acting as master can think up anything they want the others to do, within the bounds of a platonic environment. Minions spread love to other minions, as well as masters. When the minions have completed the first assignment, they return to their master for further instructions. Each person gets four minutes or so to be master, at which point the minions return to their groups to rotate leadership. Make sure that each master gets to issue at least two or three orders before rotating.

Massage Train or Circle

Have participants sit one behind the other in a row, with each person massaging the neck, shoulders, and/or back of the person in front of them. Every 60 seconds or so, the person at the very front moves to the very back. Encourage each participant to voice any touch preferences (e.g., pressure, speed, parts of body) to the person behind them, to gain practice communicating.

If there are enough people to form a relatively large circle—i.e., where each person does not have to sit at too much of an angle from the person immediately in front of them—you can have participants sit in that arrangement so nobody has to move from front to back.

You can also have people break out into pairs or small groups of three to four people, where each person has the opportunity to request what type of massage they would like from their partner(s). Time the interaction and announce when to switch, so that each person receives massage for the same amount of time.

"Touch Angel" Breakout Pods

How often do we have the opportunity to receive caring physical touch from several people at once? For most of us, this doesn't happen that often. This game allows participants to experience the benefits of nurturing group touch in a very powerful way, and allows for a greater range of possibilities than massage.[40]

Ask participants to break out into small groups of three or four. One person volunteers to be the first recipient of affection from their "touch angels," or the others in their group. The recipient is allowed to request any type of non-sexual touch they wish from the others. For example, they might request that one person in the group play with their hair, another massage their shoulders, and another rub their feet. They might request that the other group members snuggle with them. They might ask everyone to tickle their arms with very light touch, or even whisper positive affirmations into each ear.

After a set amount of time, e.g., two or three minutes, signal each group to shift its focus to a new recipient. This continues until each person has had a turn as a recipient within their group.

Recipients should feel free to voice any preferences for physical touch (e.g., pressure, speed, parts of body) before and after the interaction begins, and should also feel free to communicate pleasure in whatever ways they're comfortable with.

Emphasize that everyone in each group is fully at choice at all times. Each touch angel reserves the right to say "No" or to suggest a modification if the recipient requests something that they're not comfortable giving.

It's also perfectly acceptable if the recipient wishes to have only certain member(s) of their group touch them, but not others. Remind group members not to take such things personally. For example, a recipient may be comfortable with touch from people of one sex but not another, due to events in their personal touch history. They may need time and practice to become more comfortable with others. Perhaps a group member happens to remind them of someone who has made them uncomfortable in the past.

Even if a group member is not actively participating in physical touch for all or part of the exercise, they can still play an active role by witnessing the activity, by sitting and envisioning love and other positive feelings, and by emanating their energy to the group.[41]

Encourage participants to avoid comparing themselves to other groups, as each group will differ in comfort levels and chemistry. This is not anyone's "fault." For example, one group might have one or more individuals who prefer minimal touch, while another group delves immediately into exchanging vigorous back and foot massages, with loud vocalizations of pleasure.

Group Hug

Encourage participants to come together and wrap their arms around one another in one big, happy collective caress. Just remind everyone to be gentle with those in the middle. Participants may make soft, loving sounds, or focus upon thoughts of gratitude for one another.

Eye Gazing

Even though this activity can be done without physical touch, many would consider it to be an advanced exercise. Like some of the other exercises here, it can bring up strong emotions.

While babies and their parents frequently eye gaze for extended periods as a way of bonding, we're often socialized to lessen eye contact as we grow older. We may be told, for example, that staring is impolite or aggressive, but we may receive little instruction on how it can promote connection.[42]

Like other types of contact, eye gazing is often oversexualized. If we're not actively speaking or listening, most of us rarely make eye contact with other people for more than a second or two unless we're romantically interested in them. Extended eye contact is an important and fun part of flirting and signaling physical attraction, and hopefully always will be. But that doesn't mean we need to limit it to that purpose, provided we're also communicating in other ways to avoid sending mixed messages.

Eye gazing can create a deeper sense of intimacy between people, which can make them more comfortable with other types of interaction such as physical touch. It can generate self-awareness around your comfort levels with intimacy, and with being seen. It can feel quite wonderful, but also scary, given how we're often socialized around it. Some consider eye gazing to be an extension of physical touch, especially given that it can trigger releases of some of the same "feel good" chemicals.[43] I recommend trying it with a few people yourself before attempting to facilitate it with a group.

Ask each individual to pair up with someone else, and while standing or sitting, gaze into their eyes with simple curiosity and acceptance for a short time. Even 30 seconds is plenty of time to begin with. Let participants know they are free to close their eyes or look away from the other person if they feel at all uncomfortable at any point, or if they simply want a break from the intensity of the exercise. They may also choose another part of their partner's face, such as the center of their forehead or nose, to look at.

If participants have not yet learned about concepts such as leveling, you might suggest that they stand face to face without physically touching at all. If they *have* learned about leveling, this might be an opportunity to practice. Let them know they're free to negotiate whatever level of physical contact feels comfortable for them during eye gazing, whether it's simply holding hands, placing hands on one another's knees, or not touching at all.

After the set period of time, ask participants to switch to a new partner, unless they came with a friend or significant other with whom they wish to remain paired. Have them repeat the same exercise, or mix it up a bit by extending the time from 30 to 60 seconds. If you wish, ask them to express another positive emotion, such as joy or gratitude, through their gaze. For additional intimacy, invite participants to engage in synchronized breathing with their partner.

After two or three interactions, invite participants to share what their experiences were like.

Angel Wash

Description by Amy Baker

While this can be an ice breaker, it is also a great game to end an event, since it leaves people in a very blissful state. It works best with at least 10 people, and has been done with hundreds of people at once in outdoor settings, although that takes quite a long time.

Ask participants to find a partner and stand face to face with that person holding hands, so that the group forms two lines. Pairs then drop hands, remaining close enough to touch the people who walk between the two lines.

Then one at a time, people start from the end of the line and slowly walk between the lines, with eyes open or closed. The people in the lines gently caress the person's back, head, shoulders, and face. It might be fun to include back scratching, a bit of shoulder massage, etc., as the people pass. If the person's eyes are closed, the angels (people in the lines) guide them along as well. If you want to build group trust, encourage people to try it with eyes closed.

As soon as the first person has gotten a few feet down the line, the next can enter the line, so that there is a steady stream of people receiving touch from the angels on either side. As people enter the line, the two lines need to move a bit to fill in the empty space, to avoid ending up with a clump of people at one end of the room.

Encourage people to go through the angel wash twice, as it's nice to repeat the experience. Remind people to go slowly and really let themselves receive and take in the touch.

10 Sensitive Stuff: Sex, Culture, Dating, Diversity

"As a woman without a partner whose primary love language is physical touch, I find snuggling one of the best ways to feel connected to myself and others in a safe way. I've made great friendships along the way, too!"

—*C. E. A., age 51*

As mentioned earlier, this book includes information that you might never need, but that is nonetheless important. You don't want to get taken off guard by unforeseen issues, especially if you're facilitating more public events. Some of the information in the next two chapters fits this description.

Trying to cover all these topics in detail with your snuggle community would probably be overwhelming, but you might cover some of them briefly at your orientation event, on your group's website, or in more depth at a discussion-oriented event. Mainly, just having the knowledge yourself as a facilitator will be helpful to your group. If some members of your group want to take their snuggle awareness and skills to the next level, you can always encourage them to read this book, too![44]

Touch has the potential to bring up emotions, attitudes, and cultural factors. As you host events, you'll stretch your own boundaries a bit. Snuggle parties can provide an opportunity to explore dynamics that already impact your everyday life, but that our culture often keeps hush-hush.

We are all exposed to societal messages that impact our ability to meet our touch needs, so most of us have to undergo some reprogramming as we learn to fully enjoy snuggle parties. This reprogramming is usually well worth it, as the experiences further rewire our hearts and minds, healing attitudes that stand in our way.

As *Vitamin T* co-author Bob Czimbal explains, when two people are lying side by side at a snuggle, two different cultures are also lying next to one another. Each individual has a unique touch history. That history includes a range of people and events that affect that person's touch-related perceptions and behavior.

Following are several such issues that can impact snuggle parties. I withhold most suggestions for addressing them until the next chapter. This is to avoid repetition, because some of the solutions address several potential issues simultaneously.

Sensuality versus Sexuality with Multiple People

Because touch is often oversexualized, some people fear that snuggling with multiple people may suggest that they also want to be romantically involved with multiple people. They may avoid snuggling out of fear that they'll be viewed as promiscuous or slutty. If they're in a romantic relationship, they might fear judgment and insecurity from their partner. In the next chapter we'll cover how to draw a clearer distinction between sensuality and sexuality, which can help to address such fears.

Homophobia and Transphobia

Many people are afraid to share extended nourishing touch, such as snuggling or massage, with others of the same sex. This is particularly true of men, probably partially due to the fact that men are socialized to connect most forms of gentle physical touch with romantic interest. Thus, many men don't feel comfortable sharing with each other the same range of physical contact that many women do.

Add to the mix homophobia and transphobia, which can collectively refer to the irrational fear or hatred of people who identify as, or appear to be, one or more of the following: lesbian, gay, bisexual, transgender, queer, intersex, or asexual (LGBTQIA).[45] This often translates into avoidance of any behavior that a person fears might make them appear to fit one of these categories.

Many people may fear snuggling with anyone who doesn't fit the sex and gender category that they're sexually attracted to. For example, a heterosexual man may be comfortable snuggling only with people who are clearly biologically female, who seem to have been so since birth, and who present themselves in a very female way. On the surface, he may fear that someone in any other category might be sexually attracted to him, and will somehow try to seduce him. But deeper down, he may be afraid that snuggling with such a person will actually feel good, and fears what this would say about him. Would it mean he's also sexually attracted to that person, and is therefore bisexual or gay?

We'll look at key distinctions that can address some of these fears in the next chapter. In addition to being irrational, this type of fear also has a sad irony: One openly gay male who attends many touch-positive events told me he's encountered many gay men seeking settings where they can experience touch without it being sexualized.

It's helpful to know that fears of same-sex touch are not universal across ages and cultures. In a 2014 British study of 40 white college-aged male athletes, 37 reported having cuddled with another male on a couch or bed, and 39 reported having slept in the same bed with another male at least once since in college.[46] In the 1970s, C.A. Tripp described several cultures where men regularly engaged in a range of same-sex touch, such as alternating between all-male sleeping tents and tents where they slept with their female counterparts.[47]

I continue to learn much about myself in this area. While some snugglers aim for total neutrality regarding the sex and gender identity of the people they snuggle with, I'll be honest that I still have a preference for female snuggling energy. I simply want to be able to enjoy nourishing touch with other individuals as well, and to do so in a relaxed way. Just a few years ago, I probably wouldn't have been willing to do this at all. Through snuggle events, I've already gained much practice. So be gentle on yourself if you're currently far from neutral in your snuggling preferences; just do your best to learn and grow, and encourage others to do the same.

Sex Imbalance

Here the term *sex* refers to a person's female or male biological sex, and *sex imbalance* refers to a discrepancy in the number of females versus males attending an event.[48]

Some participants may actually enjoy a significant sex imbalance at snuggles—they may enjoy having an overabundance of individuals of a given sex to snuggle with. Others, including individuals whose identities do not neatly line up with sex categories, may find this a moot point. For some people, however, significant imbalances can pose concerns.

A few facilitators have noted that snuggle events often attract significantly more men than women, when no efforts are made to balance. This may occur partially because men often have more issues getting touch needs met in general, and may more actively seek out such events. It may occur partially because women fear that there will be "creepy men" running sexual energy, and may be shy about attending. This fear is not totally unjustified, as the majority of women have experienced sexual harassment at some point in their lives.

If men significantly outnumber women at a snuggle party, women may feel they're expected to do a favor or "take one for the team" for certain men simply because the men aren't comfortable snuggling with other men. Or, they may even feel unsafe or overpowered. This can lead to a downward spiral, where women are even less likely to attend events in the future, further exacerbating sex imbalance.

Depending upon the dynamics of your community and social circles, it is also possible that significantly more women than men will attend a given event, due to factors like homophobia being greater among men. However, a surplus of women is less likely to pose issues given that women tend to be more comfortable snuggling with each other.

Past Abuse and "Predator/Prey" Dynamics

Many people, especially women, have experienced some type of sexual or other physical abuse. Some may attend snuggle parties because their emotional scars make it challenging to obtain safe and healthy touch in other settings and relationships. Whatever the severity and surrounding circumstances of the traumatic event(s), touch that seems benign to others might trigger unexpected emotions and strong reactions for them.

In some cases, past trauma or abuse, either physical or emotional, may make a person likely to act in a "predator" or "prey" fashion.[49] In such cases, they may inadvertently behave in a way that tends to attract the opposite. An example would be a woman who speaks in a meek and withdrawn fashion, and who communicates no boundaries around how she wishes to be touched. If there also happens to be a male present who hasn't yet learned to negotiate boundaries in a healthy way, he may be attracted to her lack of confidence, and interact with her in ways that make her feel uncomfortable.

Some individuals may experience difficulties with touch due to what is essentially societal-level emotional abuse. Many LGBTQIA people suffer a range of impacts stemming from internalized homophobia, i.e., turning society's fear and hatred of them inward toward themselves. The resulting shame about one's sexual desires may lead to self-isolation from other types of physical affection as well. This may be even more likely if one's immediate family hasn't been supportive of their identity.

Couples and Dating

For most people, the idea of attending an event that is sensual but non-sexual will be a new concept. Prior to attending my first snuggle, I was very skeptical about the idea. Because I had never experienced such an event, I assumed that the real reason most people attended snuggles was just to find people to date or hook up with.

Even when snuggle events are completely platonic, there won't always be a total black-and-white distinction between platonic snuggle friends and potential romantic interests. Some people do meet future significant others and lovers at snuggle events. After finding they resonate with each other while snuggling, they mutually decide they'd like to get to know each other better outside the snuggle setting. It could even happen to you!

Indeed, snuggling can provide a relatively safe way to "feel out someone's vibe" beyond what is possible in many other social settings. Participants can explore a range of physical contact with the emotional safety net of knowing that things won't turn sexual in that setting. As one experienced female snuggler explains, "I love snuggle parties. It is the easiest, most natural way to meet people and assess right away if you are compatible with them. I met two people at snuggle parties whom I ended up dating, including my current partner."

This has a potentially risky flip side, though. The chemicals produced by snuggling can be emotionally intoxicating, and this can impair judgment slightly. Veteran snuggler Amy Baker describes what she calls the "tenth date effect." You may feel like you've been on several "regular" dates with a person, and know them relatively well, as a result of simply having cuddled with them for a while. But all you *really* know is that they feel comfortable to snuggle with, and you may have some clues as to your potential physical compatibility. Outside of that, even if you spent a decent amount of time talking, you may not know much more about them than you might have learned on the average first or second date. Hanging out with them one-on-one could be very different than hanging out with them in the group snuggle setting.

Your events may also include participants who are already in romantic relationships, and who attend with their existing significant other(s). Even a non-sexual but touch-positive event like a snuggle can trigger insecurities for a couple who has not candidly discussed their boundaries and preferences before an event. Additionally, some participants may experience uncertainty around what is on- or off-limits with someone who is in a romantic relationship, especially if that person's significant other is also present.

While this may sound like a lot to be concerned about, we'll cover some practices to address these issues in the next chapter.

Neurodiversity

Neurodiversity is "a concept where neurological differences are to be recognized and respected as any other human variation."[50] It is often utilized by individuals who are relatively high-functioning in many areas of their life—sometimes even functioning well above average in certain areas such as intellectual capacity—but who have neurological variations that still make their life challenging in certain ways.

Particularly if your events are open to the public, you may occasionally encounter neurodiverse individuals who have difficulty meeting intimacy needs in everyday settings due to their variation(s), and who seek snuggle groups for comfort and support.

There's not space here to cover all the possibilities, but I'll provide one example that seems to be relatively common. In addition to having a close family member with the variation, I've met several people at snuggle events who are open about having Asperger Syndrome, or Asperger's. As the American Psychological Association recently incorporated it into "Autism Spectrum Disorder," it may also be viewed as a high-functioning form of autism, without intellectual or language deficits.[51] People may vary in terms of whether they prefer to say they have Asperger's or autism, and some may object to the term *disorder*.

It's important not to overgeneralize, as each person with Asperger's is different. That being said, a few characteristics

are relatively common and helpful to be aware of. Some people with Asperger's take rules very literally, so once ground rules or preferences have been explicitly communicated, they're likely to make good efforts to follow them. On the other hand, they don't always capture or convey the more nuanced communication that many people rely upon to convey wants and needs. This can include differences in eye contact and body language, and an inability to understand some humor that may make them seem insensitive when they're not. They may simply require more explicit verbal expressions and requests.[52]

Physiological Diversity

At snuggle parties, as in any environment, you will encounter people with a range of physiological conditions and abilities. Some of this is due to natural processes such as aging, and some may be due to differences in health, recent injuries, illness, or other conditions. In fact, some individuals may seek out snuggle parties because their physical condition makes it difficult to get touch needs met in other ways, or because the soothing aspects of snuggling help with pain and physical stress relief.

A person's physical composition will impact what types of snuggling and touch-based interactions they're comfortable participating in, and the types of fluff they're comfortable snuggling on.

Demographic Differences

People of different racial and ethnic backgrounds, countries, geographic regions, spiritual or religious practices, and ages may have cultural differences around communication and touch. These differences may include what types of touch feel comfortable versus invasive, and how they're used to communicating and negotiating around touch-based interactions. Sometimes, very strong historical factors can play a role in our touch-related wants, needs, and behaviors.

Because we don't have space to cover every possible difference here, we'll examine just one powerful example to illustrate: the unfortunate legacy of the slavery era in the U.S. During that time, many white people claimed total ownership over black people's bodies, including how long they worked, how they ate, and how they were touched. Sometimes black people were even showcased in zoos. Their bodies were violated in numerous ways, often even when they weren't officially enslaved. There's at least one documented account of two white men forcing an enslaved male and "free" black female to have sex at gunpoint while they watched.[53]

Such horrific events created trauma that most of us cannot imagine, and the wounds continue to heal today. Liz Dwyer, a black woman who writes on social justice and sustainability topics, explains how a white woman she didn't know approached her at the pool and asked if she could touch her hair. When Dwyer told her "No," the woman didn't just politely walk away. She instead requested an explanation, and became upset after Dwyer didn't say anything, wondering why letting her touch her hair was such a big deal.

Dwyer didn't feel that she owed the woman any explanation, but shares some of the reasons that ran through her head: "You're a stranger...I'm not an animal in a zoo...This is my body...My black ancestors may have been your ancestors' property, and had to smile while they got touched in ways they didn't want to, but I am not YOUR property."

While the white woman probably felt she was initially acting with good intentions, conflict occurred after she refused to accept another person's touch-related boundaries, and seemed to take "No" personally. Dwyer had many valid reasons for saying "No"—big reasons that most people would probably rather not discuss while trying to relax at the pool. But the white woman probably didn't have the same type and degree of touch-based trauma in her ancestry as Dwyer did, and her own racial group had always held a position of greater power, so she had probably never given as much thought to such things. Actually, she had the privilege of not *having* to think as much about such things.

Truth be told, as a white male, I had never previously given much thought to this specific topic either. I realized that my ignorance ran even deeper after reading a bit more and mentioning the articles to a friend with experience in salons. I hadn't realized that many black women are hesitant to touch their *own* hair after having it done—often in ways to conform to the dominant white-centric standard of beauty—as it often has a very delicate hold and can be difficult and expensive to fix.[54]

This is just one example of how cultural differences—and sometimes even simple physiological differences—can impact our views and behaviors around touch, in ways we may be completely unaware of. Whatever a snuggler's cultural identity, they may say "No" to certain touch requests for reasons rooted in social power dynamics, historical injustices, and other cultural factors. Sometimes they may openly share their reasons, but probably only if they believe others are open-minded enough to hear them without attacking. In many cases someone may not want to take on a "cultural educator" role, and may simply want to relax and snuggle like everyone else.

11 Options for Addressing the Sensitive Stuff

"Before I became a snuggler, the only option available to address my craving for intimate human connection seemed to be coital sex. Now I can meet my needs to be touched in a variety of ways. The touch provided by snuggling has become a major source of connection and pleasure for me, plus it produces many fewer undesirable side effects."

—B. B., age 63

Now that we've covered some of the sexual, cultural, and psychological issues that may arise, let's discuss possibilities for preventing and handling some of them. As with the previous chapter, there's some information here that may be helpful for you to share with participants, and there are some concepts that will benefit your group merely by your understanding them in case they're ever needed.

To a large extent, it's up to you and other facilitators to determine how inclusive you're willing and able to be with your events. If you feel very anxious around people who have differences you're not accustomed to, including any of the characteristics described earlier, you might wish to begin with smaller, private events including only people you know. You can always expand as you become more comfortable as a facilitator.

Host Orientation Events

It's up to you whether you require an orientation for new snugglers. It may not be necessary if you host private events primarily for friends and their guests, but if your group is open to the general public, such a requirement has a few benefits.

First, you can include some of the conversation topics and games from the "Connective Games and Activities" chapter, where there is also a sample orientation event agenda. This ensures that snugglers are starting out with at least a basic level of shared understanding and education. Secondly, covering ground rules and important concepts in more detail at an orientation enables you to use a more summarized explanation at the beginning of each snuggle. You're not always having to expound just for new participants.

Thirdly, required orientations can lessen the likelihood of certain dynamics such as "predator/prey" described earlier. They can empower individuals with additional behavioral tools and awareness, including asking permission, saying "No," and setting boundaries in a healthier and more confident way. Additionally, they send the message that everyone's safety and personal empowerment is taken seriously. Orientations may serve a participant screening function as well. Individuals who have no desire to learn healthier new behaviors may not be willing to attend a required orientation; this in turn, would preclude attendance at regular snuggles for them.

Discuss Sensuality versus Sexuality Distinctions

A few concepts and resources are particularly helpful to cover during orientation events for new snugglers. The first is the distinction between *sensuality* and *sexuality*. Sensual touch can feel good in many ways, and can include playing with hair, lightly touching another person's face, and sharing a foot, shoulder, back, or neck massage. However, there is no reason that it needs to lead to sex, or needs to be enjoyed only with romantic partners. Sure, you may connect with someone at a snuggle with whom you mutually resonate on a deeper level, and later decide to become intimately involved with outside that setting, but that's just icing on the cake.

The following table, from *Vitamin T: A Guide to Healthy Touch*, outlines the differences between sensual and sexual touch.[55]

Sensual Touch	Sexual Touch
relaxing	exciting
friendly	romantic
public	private
normal sensitivity	heightened sensitivity
affectionate	passionate
all ages	adults only
general permission	specific permission
clothes on	clothes off
no genital contact	genital contact
feels pleasant	feels erotic
minimal skin contact	maximum skin contact
releases tension	releases sex hormones
non-aerobic	aerobic and anaerobic

Once we grasp the distinction between sensuality and sexuality, we can understand how one doesn't necessarily need to lead to the other. Then we can understand how we can be *pansensual* (enjoying sensual but non-sexual touch that is not limited by one's own or others' biological sex, gender, or gender identity), regardless of whom we prefer to have sex with.[56] And regardless of whom the person we're snuggling with prefers to have sex with. You can be pansensual regardless of whether your sexual orientation is homosexual, heterosexual, bisexual, pansexual, asexual, etc.[57]

This distinction can help to diminish some of the dynamics related to homophobia and transphobia. Above all, it's important to create an environment where people can be honest without any personal attacks or vocal judgments of others.

Another important related distinction is that of *polysensuality* versus *polysexuality*.[58] In some cases, as a person becomes more comfortable sharing platonic sensual touch with a range of people, they may also become more curious about sharing romantic and/or sexual connections with multiple people. However, this is not true for everyone. Connecting with more than one person through pleasurable platonic touch does not necessarily mean we also want or need to be sexual with more than one person.

We may choose to have one person to whom we limit our romantic and sexual involvement, while still having other friends with whom we connect on a deeper-than-average— but still platonic—level through snuggling, massage trades, and similar activities. Such arrangements are often entirely off limits in romantic relationships, out of the misunderstanding that they must be linked to sexual connection.

When we exchange touch, we are essentially sharing loving energy with other people. If done in a caring way that includes open communication with our romantic partner, agreements that allow each person to feel safe, and consent from everyone involved, it needn't pose a threat to our romantic relationships.

Clarify Feminine and Masculine Coexistence

Some people may continue to insist that activities like snuggling are just for women, even though we all need nurturing touch from the day we're born. They may fear that snuggling will make a man less masculine and less attractive. Most women and men who are open-minded enough to come to an event will already see beyond such attitudes to some extent. However, they may still be wrestling with deeply embedded cultural programming.

In such cases, it may be helpful to emphasize a point that's not always apparent: Regardless of how "feminine" someone considers snuggling to be, it doesn't impact someone's masculinity. Femininity and masculinity are not mutually exclusive. Expressing more of one does not equate to less of the other. In fact, being able to embody both can make a person seem both stronger *and* more attractive.

Ask a heterosexual man to consider a female actress he considers to be both feminine and attractive, who has also starred in at least one action or adventure role he's familiar with. Did seeing her engaged in more aggressive and "masculine" activities detract from her femininity or attractiveness? He'll most likely say "No." Likewise, ask a heterosexual woman if seeing a man snuggling with a baby, still viewed by many as a feminine behavior, makes him seem any less masculine or attractive. Likewise, she'll probably say "No."[59]

A visual resource that may help with this type of discussion is "The Genderbread Person," viewable online at itspronouncedmetrosexual.com. It illustrates how *feminine* and *masculine* are not mutually exclusive, and how the ways we choose to express ourselves can be independent of our sexual orientation and physical sex.

Discuss and Validate Cultural Differences

In an introductory or orientation session, you might encourage snugglers to share significant ways in which they believe their culture has influenced their touch preferences. Are there ways in which they sense they may differ from others in the group? Don't single out a participant just because they're of a different race, age group, nationality, or other demographic category, but invite discussion as part of a broad conversation including all types of cultural differences.

One thing is very important to emphasize in such conversations: *each type of cultural influence is equally valid, and unique to each person.* This is true whether the cultural influence has to do with race, ethnicity, sex, gender, spirituality or religion, age, socioeconomic status, and so on.

In facilitating any discussions, also keep in mind that two cultural influences may share similarities, but that does not make them identical. A deep or even first-hand understanding of one group's experience may enhance someone's empathy, but it does not equate to a full understanding of the other group. For example, both black people and women have been oppressed in many ways, and have had to fight for equal rights in the U.S. They have both been victims of physical and emotional violence, which might impact touch-related preferences in some similar ways. However, there are also many differences in the nature of the oppression each group has faced.

Along the same lines, trying to determine which person in a conversation has experienced greater disadvantage or oppression is seldom fruitful. It can convert an otherwise constructive conversation into an "Oppression Olympics," where two or more people become increasingly agitated as each attempts to convey that their group has faced the greatest injustices. For example, a white woman and black man might debate whether the disadvantages of being female or being black have had a greater impact on their touch preferences. The truth is that sex and race simply have *different* profound impacts, some of which may be stronger than others. Additionally, those impacts will be different for each woman, for each black person, and for each individual who fits both of these categories.

Emphasize Clear Communication Responsibility

Participants need to understand that it is ultimately their responsibility to communicate clearly what they do and don't want in any given interaction. Because each person has different cultural influences and touch histories, only they can accurately convey their own touch-related wants via a "Yes," "No," or leveling in any given moment. At the same time, if they find themselves unclear about another person's preferences, it's safer to ask rather than rely upon assumptions.

Practicing clearer and more literal expression can also improve interactions with individuals who may have more difficulty with social nuances in general, e.g., individuals with neurological variations like Asperger's. If your group includes such individuals, it may be especially helpful to remind everyone of the benefits of improved communication across the board—with *any* relatively new person in a snuggle-related setting.

Consider having a universal "I don't want to be touched right now" gesture that everyone in your group is familiar with. My favorite is the "sanctuary gesture" mentioned earlier in the sample ground rules list, and illustrated again in the following photo.

To form the sanctuary gesture, you simply cross your arms over your chest with your palms facing yourself. Created by the authors of *Vitamin T*, it has already become popular among dance and touch-positive events in Portland. This is a very efficient way of communicating. It saves effort for the person employing it, and also for others who might otherwise approach them with a snuggle request.

Clear communication also includes making known any physical limitations that may impact a person's snuggling experience, or that might affect how others should interact with them. For example, if a guest has a sore knee from a recent injury, and doesn't want anyone placing pressure on it, they should make that clearly known to others before snuggling. Or, if someone has a physical limitation that makes it more comfortable for them to sit upright rather than lying down, they should let the group know this so they can reserve a spot on the couch, love seat, or chair.

Speaking of physical injuries, anytime you're hosting an event in your home, it's wise to make sure you have either home owner's or renter's insurance that covers accidental injuries to guests. While the chances of sustaining a significant injury while snuggling are slim, accidents like slipping on icy stairs while entering or exiting can be more serious.

Emphasize Respect of Boundaries

As mentioned in the ground rules, no one is obligated to give an explanation when they say "No." This is helpful in cases where someone may not feel comfortable with a given interaction due to cultural reasons, or reasons stemming from their personal touch history, that may be difficult to explain. Remind participants that when they hear a "No," not to take it personally, and not to badger the other person for an explanation. If the person saying "No" wants to provide a teaching moment, it's up to them to do so voluntarily.

Play Educational Games

While we can learn a lot through reading a book, having a conversation, or listening to someone lecture, it's also important to learn through interacting, feeling, and experiencing with the body. For example, if someone is terrified at the prospect of snuggling with people who wear purple shirts, he may need to start by simply experiencing a brief hug or shoulder massage from someone wearing a purple shirt. If someone lacks confidence in their ability to maintain safe boundaries and communicate their preferences during a snuggle, they may develop confidence through actually practicing with other people at an introductory training event. Some of the interactive exercises in the "Connective Games and Activities" chapter may be helpful.

Sex Balance—or Not

Sex balancing means taking intentional steps to make the number of biologically female and male attendees at any given event roughly equal.[60] For example, if five women and seven men have RSVP'd for an event, then two of the men may be excluded unless two more women RSVP. Sex balancing can avoid some of the issues that occur when there are many more men. As noted earlier, there may occasionally be more women, but the issues may be less pronounced because women are often more comfortable snuggling with each other.

Sex balancing will usually take additional effort on your part, and it may discourage some participants. You'll need to monitor your RSVP list actively as the date approaches, and then either turn people away or try to persuade a few friends of the underrepresented sex to attend at the last minute. You can place some of the responsibility in the laps of participants, guaranteeing people a spot if they bring a lover, platonic friend, colleague, or even family member of the other sex.

Ultimately, these approaches tend to exclude some of the people who probably stand to benefit the most from participating—i.e., those whose social connections are currently limited for whatever reason. However, at the same time, you want to make sure your other participants are feeling comfortable and getting their needs met as well. So it's up you to strike a balance, and if necessary you can ask your most active participants what they're most comfortable with.

If you want additional perspective on this topic, TribalLove.net also has some resources for building balanced guest lists.

Even perfect sex balancing won't address all related needs and concerns. Not everyone is heterosexual, and not everyone fits or agrees with binary female/male categorization. Furthermore, at an event with only non-sexual touch, should sex or sexual orientation even be relevant? Having a sex imbalance may actually provide participants—especially males—with opportunities to grow and stretch their snuggle boundaries. I've had this experience myself, as I'm still becoming more comfortable snuggling with other men, and allowing myself to give and receive nurturing energy.

If you hold introductory orientation sessions for your group, you can cover key points from earlier sections in this chapter: "Discuss Sensuality versus Sexuality Distinctions" and "Clarify Feminine and Masculine Coexistence." You might openly discuss the fact that when men are willing to snuggle only with women, women sometimes feel overwhelmed and discouraged from attending events. That will at least increase awareness about these issues.

If you don't include an opportunity to snuggle at the end of orientation events, limiting activities to facilitated games, you'll have little reason to be concerned with sex balancing. This will enable you to be as inclusive as possible at your orientation events, regardless of how you manage your snuggle parties. This is a practice that Oregon Touch has adopted.[61] It's one way to prevent women from feeling overwhelmed by an overabundance of needy-feeling men wanting to snuggle with them (and refusing to snuggle with other men) at they very first event they attend.

If you're male, and you're having difficulty getting many women to attend your events, you might occasionally ask a woman to co-facilitate with you. This may help women to feel more comfortable even if the event isn't balanced, and it may also help you to stay informed about dynamics impacting participants of the other sex. Some women may feel more comfortable sharing candid feedback about sex- and gender-related issues with a woman, just as men may feel more comfortable sharing with another man.

In the next section we'll cover a few more approaches that aim to ensure everyone gets some attention, even when there's not perfect sex balance.

Encourage Snuggling with Many People

At any given snuggle, participants will have different intentions depending upon their individual needs and comfort levels. Some snugglers may be willing to spend some or most of their time reaching out to those who appear to need touch the most, regardless of how familiar or similar they are. Others may prefer to connect only with people already familiar to them, people who are attractive to them, or people who similar to them in terms of age, sex, race, and so on.

These differences are human nature. I'll be the first to admit that once I've established a comfortable "snuggle bond" with someone, I'm excited to see them at events, and I'll usually try to spend some time with them. Also, I won't deny that there's a bit of added fun in snuggling with someone I happen to find physically attractive, even while keeping in mind that snuggle parties are not the place to express or act upon such opinions. As mentioned earlier, many people develop close bonds, and often end up being good friends outside the snuggle setting as well.

However, if everyone always sticks to their familiar and favorite snuggle buddies, newcomers may have a difficult time fitting in. Many people will feel especially touch deprived at their first event or two—probably their main reason for joining the group—and might initially appear to others as overly needy or awkward. Unless they have charisma or physical attractiveness to compensate, they might not initially seem to be the most attractive snuggle partner on the surface.

No one should ever be forced to "take one for the team," or to snuggle with someone who is giving off vibes that make them uncomfortable. Also, everyone should still have time to cater to their own needs and snuggle with their favorites. However, if each established snuggler is willing to spend even a small portion of their time with a new, different, shy, or seemingly alone participant, then new participants will feel more included and will be more likely to pay it along in the future.

Due to the snuggle party "tenth date effect" discussed earlier under "Couples and Dating," there's a strong tendency for people to develop favorites after interacting only one or two times. This makes it even more important to encourage mixing things up sometimes.

There are a few ways to mix things up, as demonstrated by Kristen Reynolds of Oregon Touch. You can make it a point to switch snuggle partners yourself once or twice during each event, at which time you gently encourage others to do the same. Also, you can encourage a few enthusiastic snugglers to be "snuggle ambassadors," striving to be as inclusive as possible, and setting a good example for others with their snuggle behavior. This can include switching partners so they're spending at least part of their snuggle time with a newcomer. It can include demonstrating a willingness to snuggle with people of any sex and gender identity, regardless of their own sex and orientation.

The Blind Test

You can even list members who have pledged to be snuggle ambassadors on your group's website, to give a bit of extra recognition, and to remind newcomers and relatively shy snugglers that they're not alone. You might also give them some type of tag or bracelet to wear at events.

Have a Reporting System for Unsafe Behavior

In an environment where expectations are clearly outlined, and where participants are comfortable communicating when something uncomfortable happens, the occasional would-be predatory or insensitive person is more likely to be discouraged. Let participants know how to contact you either during or after the event if they feel someone is behaving inappropriately.

You don't want to make participants feel unsafe, as the vast majority of people don't pose a threat. But somewhere on your website or official materials, make it clear that you reserve the right to temporarily or permanently restrict a member's participation if you have good reason to believe their actions are making others feel unsafe.

It's up to you how specific you wish to be regarding any advertised policies, versus determining what actions are most appropriate on a case-by-case basis. If you form a group that has multiple facilitators, make sure you have a system for alerting each other about any potential concerns.

Communicate Dating Guidelines

As mentioned earlier, some people have met romantic partners and soul mates at snuggle events. It might even happen to you. There's nothing inherently wrong with this; when such life-enhancing connections happen without negatively impacting the dynamics of the group, that's awesome. Icing on the cake. Just keep in mind that when events are announced as being sensual but non-sexual in nature, maintaining a safe container is vital. This enables participants to relax, explore, and connect comfortably.

While you don't want to overpolice, you may wish to suggest guidelines that discourage participants from viewing events as pick-up environments. For example, it's probably a good idea to discourage compliments of a sexual nature. You might suggest that it's okay for participants to offer their own contact info to others, but that it's not okay to request others' contact info from them. That way, two people have a way of getting in touch if they're mutually interested in connecting further; but if someone is not interested, it's totally acceptable to say "No." Remind participants that if a romantic connection ends in an awkward breakup, it may have a lasting impact on both people if they continue to see each other at future snuggle events.

Additionally, you might inform participants that the chemicals produced by snuggling can be emotionally intoxicating, and that this can impair judgment slightly. Tell them about the "tenth date effect" discussed in the previous chapter under "Couples and Dating," and remind them that just because someone feels comfortable to snuggle with in a group setting doesn't necessarily mean they'll feel safe and comfortable to be alone with in an outside setting.

Beyond providing such information, you have no control over participants' choices outside the event settings. People ultimately need to take responsibility for themselves around exchanging contact info and relating outside of the group snuggle setting. However, if someone feels that they're being harassed at events or on your group's website (e.g., a message or discussion board), you may need to take action.

Offer These Tips to Couples

Your events may attract participants who are already in romantic relationships. They might attend with or without their significant other(s). You can share some of the following ideas with them, or direct them to this book for the finer details. These ideas are geared toward those who are presently committed to a relationship, versus those attending snuggle parties to help them transition out of a relationship.

As mentioned under "Why Should You Be Throwing Snuggle Parties?" earlier, snuggle parties can enhance the connection between two people currently in a romantic relationship. On a few occasions, I've experienced intensified attraction with my partner shortly after we both had a fun and nourishing time at a snuggle party.

However, enjoying such benefits generally requires a couple to do some initial homework. Even though they're non-sexual in nature, snuggle parties can still trigger challenging emotions and feelings including insecurity. It's impossible to plan for all possibilities, but a couple can greatly increase their odds of having nourishing experiences by discussing concerns, wants, and expectations with each another before an event.

Here are a few questions romantic partners might discuss before a snuggle:

- How much time, if any, do we want to spend snuggling with each other, versus snuggling with other people?

- Are there any ways in which you're not okay with me touching other people, or with them touching me?

- How often should we check in with each other to make sure we're both feeling safe and comfortable?

- What is our method for checking in with each other? For example, are there signals we can use to let the other one know if we're okay or if we need to talk?

- What shifts in our behavior are we willing to make if one of us indicates they are not okay?

- Should we place any limits on the time we can spend snuggling with any one person?

- Is it okay for me to snuggle with another woman when you're not also directly snuggling with me as part of the same group? Another man?

Especially after their first snuggle or two, couples should talk with each other very honestly about any concerns that arose for either of them. Each one needs to be willing to accept the other's experience as valid and understandable, and to try to avoid blaming.

The first time I witnessed my partner snuggling with another man for an extended period, I experienced insecurity. At the end of the event, my partner and the man she had been snuggling with for a while (what I perceived as a very long while) approached me at the snack table. They were both very rosy-cheeked with a blissed out look in their eyes. Oxytocin at work, to be sure! At that moment, the two of them seemed so into each other that I worried I might have romantic competition. My insecurity was magnified by having had a less satisfactory snuggle experience, as I was feeling a bit introverted that evening. After my partner and I had a somewhat challenging but very honest conversation about it, I felt both reassured and closer to her. Subsequent snuggle events seemed more fun and relaxed for both of us.

The fact is that most people who attend snuggle parties will find other people they enjoy snuggling with, and will form some level of bond with them. Also, most people will sometimes snuggle with others they find physically attractive, and with others who find them physically attractive. There's nothing inherently wrong with any of this, provided it isn't violating one's relationship agreements, and isn't decreasing one's availability and energy for intimacy with their own partner.

It's important for both partners to feel that participation in snuggling complements the overall physical and emotional intimacy they already share with each other, and does not substitute for, replace, or distract from it. Neither person should leave their partner doubting that they remain their favorite physical intimacy companion, even as new friends are made at snuggle parties.[62]

At a snuggle party, each member of a couple should be responsible for communicating directly with other snugglers about what types of touch they are okay with. Couples should not draw other snugglers into their dynamics, or expect other snugglers to automatically treat them any specific way just because they're in a romantic relationship. Following are two examples.

Example #1: Dick decides that he still isn't comfortable with Jane being spooned by other men, and Jane agrees to say "No" to any spooning requests from men for the next three events. At snuggle events, it's up to Jane to let other men know this directly herself. Other participants shouldn't be expected to figure this out, or to look to Dick to communicate what Jane can and cannot do.

Example #2: Two hours into a snuggle party, Dick is still snuggling one-on-one with the same woman he started with. Jane feels upset because she and Dick had agreed to avoid snuggling with the same person one-on-one for more than roughly an hour. Jane should politely ask Dick if he has a moment to talk so they can have a conversation in private, away from the rest of the snugglers. Neither of them should triangulate the other snuggler into their conversation. She may know nothing about Jane and Dick's agreement.

Promote Awareness of Supports

Your events will attract people with a broad range of comfort levels around physical touch. Many will be looking to increase their capacity for physical affection. You may encounter individuals who are looking for a safe setting where they can overcome impacts of physical abuse and trauma. While you want to be as compassionate as possible, remember that you're not responsible for providing in-depth counseling, or for providing a therapy or support group—and neither are your other participants.

If a snuggler seems to be emotionally triggered frequently, let them know you want the best for them, and ask whether they can communicate their boundaries and needs in a way that enables them to feel safe. If they cannot, even after any orientation or training you require of participants, you might encourage them to consider a counselor or support group for additional self-care. Or, invite them to organize a snuggle event that would better fit their current needs—for example, a women's-only or men's-only snuggle party or discussion—and offer to provide some support in planning or advertising the event if you have time.

Your orientation events can also encourage use of peer support. For example, participants might pledge that they won't give in to peer pressure when it comes to setting and maintaining touch boundaries.[63] Each person chooses one or two one or two "peer support partners." They agree to report to each other after attending snuggle parties, regarding how well they honored their personal boundaries.

You might also keep a list of a few local professionals you can easily access if a participant asks for a referral to a therapist or support group. One broader example is the "First Call for Help" social services referral number and website that United Way has catalyzed in many communities.

Consider a Liability Waiver and Agreement

None of the information in this book is a replacement for professional legal advice. It is your responsibility to be aware of any laws or legal guidelines that may impact you. Laws vary by location and situation, and evolve over time. Recommendations here are not guaranteed to provide legal protection. If in doubt, consult with a local attorney.

That being said, you may wish to create a form that each new group member is required to sign following an orientation, prior to attending other events. This is particularly the case if you're creating a group or events that will be open to the larger public.

A liability waiver and agreement form is a way of ensuring that participants are providing informed consent, while outlining some boundaries and responsibilities. It provides a signed acknowledgement that they understand and agree to the most important rules. It clarifies that there is some risk inherent in attending events, even though you strive to make them as safe as possible. Assuming it is written in accordance with your location's laws, it may also help to protect you and others who catalyze events, should one of the following occur:

- You decide to ban a troublesome person as a protective measure, and they seek retribution out of anger.
- A participant blames you for harm suffered as a direct or indirect consequence of attending one of your events.
- A participant files legal charges against another participant due to an interaction during an event. The defendant claims that event organizers are responsible.

These are just a few possibilities. I don't want to make you paranoid, as I believe that in most cases people are reasonable and understanding. However, when you're organizing events that can trigger strong emotions, that run against currently accepted societal norms, and that provide opportunities for participants to interact in ways to which they're not accustomed, it's important that everyone involved be as informed and protected as possible.

Because the field of snuggling is relatively new, best practices surrounding these forms are still evolving. However, a few individuals and organizations listed under "Additional Resources" have created forms. Alongside consulting with a local attorney, you might look at some of theirs, and check snuggleparty.org for links.

Following are some statements you might include in a liability waiver and agreement form, borrowed largely from LoveTribe:[64]

- I certify that I am at least 18 years old, and am not acting as a media representative.[65]

- I understand that snuggle events are not a substitute for professional mental health services. Should I require such support, I am responsible for seeking it.

- I agree to maintain the confidentiality of other attendees.

- I understand that attendance and participation is always voluntary, and that I am never required to interact with anyone else without my explicit consent. I may face legal repercussions for attempting to interact with others without their consent.

- I understand I may be held liable for damages incurred in response to exposing others to communicable organisms.

- I agree to follow the event rules. I understand that I may be asked to leave for not following the rules, or for engaging in behavior otherwise deemed to be potentially harmful. I agree to inform a facilitator if I observe unsafe conditions.

- I understand that a range of risks are associated with attending and participating in snuggle events. These include: the triggering of strong emotions; physical injury or death arising from snuggling, movement, assuming different physical positions, physical interaction, and use of a range of equipment prone to possible malfunction; allergic reactions; contraction of communicable disease or organisms; and social consequences of others' failure to honor confidentiality.

- I agree to release from legal liability, and to waive my right to sue, group organizers, event planners, facilitators, volunteers, assistants, venue hosts, and property owners or tenants (collectively "Released Parties") for any damage, claim, loss, liability, or cost to people or property arising from my event attendance or participation, whether caused by the negligence of the Released Parties or otherwise.

- I assume full responsibility for risk of bodily injury, illness, psychological damage, death, or property damage to myself or others arising from my attendance or participation in snuggle-related events, whether caused by the Released Parties or otherwise. If any of the Released Parties are found liable to me, the total liability of the Released Parties liability is limited to my admission fee.

You might include a copy of event ground rules in the form, or a reference to the website where the rules are posted. You might also note that participants are responsible for keeping abreast of any changes in the rules.

Host Events Catering to Specific Demographics

Ideally, your events will attract a range of people who can openly embrace and adapt to diversity. Over time, however, as your events draw more people and increase in diversity, you might find it helpful to host snuggle events or discussion groups catering to specific populations.

Oregon Touch, for example, has hosted events for women who are shy about attending co-ed snuggles. Over time, some of those women may decide they're ready to attend co-ed events as well, and some may continue to find solace in having women's-only snuggles. Manifest Men's Wellness Group in Portland has held all-male snuggles. Such events can help to desensitize men to snuggling with others of their own sex. This, in turn, might make the co-ed events these men attend more attractive to women as well. I recently communicated with someone planning an LGBTQIA-focused snuggle group in another state.

If someone in your group wishes to host more specialized events, this can provide an opportunity to share facilitation responsibilities. If such events are advertised through the same group through which you host events, encourage consistency in the basic ground rules and expectations. This will help to avoid confusion.

Talk with Individuals One-on-One if Needed

From time to time you may encounter situations where you're uncertain of a participant's needs, where it's necessary to balance their needs with those of the group, or where your own time and energy limitations make it difficult to cater to everyone.

If this occurs, it can help to speak with a person individually to get a better understanding of their needs, in a way that doesn't put them on the spot in front of the group. This might be the case if you have a participant with a neurological variation that seems to be impacting their interactions, a guest who is experiencing strong emotional triggers, someone with a physical variation or injury, or someone who appears to be uncomfortable or distressed for unknown reasons.

If it's impossible or highly inconvenient to speak with someone in person, consider including a phone call alongside email or other text messaging. While this might sound like common sense, I mention this because it's easy to forget about the personal touch of "old fashioned" modes of communication in today's world—even when we're organizing events as personal as snuggle parties.

If your snuggle group eventually grows to where you're unable to keep up with communication, find a warm and extroverted member who would enjoy serving as the lead communicator, public relations person, community concerns contact, or some similar title.

Always Let Guests Know What to Expect

At some point down the road, you might decide that you still enjoy snuggle parties, but also want to experiment with events that allow more intimate touch. For example, you might want to host an event where people are free to remove clothing down to their underwear and exchange oil massages if they wish. You might want to host an event where people must still remain fully clothed, but are free to exchange some erotic energy through kissing.

The how-to's of such events are beyond this book's scope, as they require additional facilitation expertise. However, I list here a few important things to consider if you believe you'll eventually want to head in this direction. (If you don't, you can skip the rest of this section.) A few sources of events, coaching, and training around more intimate and erotic touch are listed under "Additional Resources."

Some of your group's participants may also wish to explore a greater range of touch, and some may not. If you begin a group with the stated intention of focusing only upon platonic snuggling, consider starting a separate group for any events that extend beyond that. Otherwise, many members of the original group may have concerns about new types of people showing up at events, whether they'll honor the ground rules, and so on. On the other hand, if you know from the outset that you eventually want to offer additional event possibilities to the same group, be up front about that from the beginning.

Where a group offers events with varying degrees of physical intimacy, it's important to have a clear system for describing the "level" of each event—i.e., what types of touch are permissible and not permissible. Such a system is vital for maintaining an environment of safety and trust. People need to know in advance what to expect; this is the foundation of informed consent.

Given the diversity of ways in which people experience and express intimacy, opinions can vary on what constitutes more "intimate" touch. The types of touch that feel platonic versus sexual can vary somewhat from person to person, and more intimate touch doesn't always mean more sexual touch. In fact, the same type of touch can take on very different meanings for two people interacting, depending upon the setting, intent, roles and relationships between the two people, and cultural backgrounds.[66] So it's important to include specific, explicit examples of the types of touch that are permitted at any event. It's even more important to remind participants that they are always at choice, however many options may be on the buffet.

Vitamin T: A Guide to Healthy Touch offers one model for organizing the range of touch types, outlining seven levels of touch. Level One, or public touch, includes introductions with handshakes. Hugging is a few levels above at Level Four or "friendly touch," and cuddling is just above that at "family touch." The highest levels, "personal touch" and "special touch," include things like bathing and sleeping together, and more intimate types of massage and dance.

Some existing groups use a numeric system for their events, where their website has clear descriptions of the types of activities one can expect at an event advertised as Level One, Level Two, Level Three, and so on. The Sex-Positive Portland Meetup group's website offers one example of this.[67] It's also possible to use playful names. TribalLove.net, for example, uses the categories Social, Snuggly, Rompy, Eros, Tantric/Temple, and Edge to denote different levels of events, which cover virtually the full spectrum of touch.

To avoid confusing people, and possibly even infringing upon copyrights or trademarks, check with any group prior to using identical names for your own events. Some groups have worked hard to develop and clarify different event categories, so that participants consistently know what to expect.

12 Self-Care: Time, Money, and De-stressing

"Snuggling helped ease my chronic pain & enriched my recovery from surgery by soothing my parasympathetic nervous system & lowering my cortisol levels."

—E. G., age 37

You're likely reading this book because, like me, you believe that snuggle parties will improve lives—not just others' lives, but yours. While as a facilitator you can't kick back and relax quite as much as attendees, you deserve to have just as much fun as everyone else at your events. You're not required to be a martyr. If you ever start to feel like one, that doesn't help anyone. Your guests will likely sense it, and they'll have more difficulty relaxing. You'll be less likely to want to continue doing events. So here are a few thoughts for taking care of yourself, lessening stress, and minimizing chances of burnout.

Decide if You Need Volunteers or Co-Organizers

In the beginning, it may be entirely up to you to get the ball rolling, creating and organizing snuggle events in your area. If you want events to happen regularly, you may want to enlist assistance. Consider how much of the following you're willing to take on yourself, versus which things you'll want help with:

- creating events and their invitations
- creating policies and ground rules, and communicating them to the group
- conducting orientations or trainings of new participants
- spreading the word: posting invitations on social networking sites, sending out email, and so on
- covering any financial costs to maintain a presence on a social networking website (some are free while others have fees)

- keeping track of RSVPs (more effort if sex balancing), collecting any contributions or admissions fees, and answering questions about a given event
- facilitating the events
- cleaning up the physical space before and after the events
- covering the up-front cost of obtaining fluff, beyond what attendees provide themselves
- covering the time and cost of maintaining fluff, such as cleaning, transporting, and storing it

For some of the above items, it may make sense to have one or more co-organizers. If you don't want to facilitate all the events, you might host and facilitate a few events with others. This will not only enable you to share the workload, but will also provide one or more learning partners with whom you can discuss what did and didn't work after each event.

After doing a few events together, you and any co-facilitators might split off to do separate events, pairing up with new facilitators who want to gain experience. Eventually, you'll have a small group of people who are all capable of hosting their own events. If you end with at least four such people, each of whom is willing to host roughly one event per month, then you'll have one snuggle event per week going on in your area!

Even if you don't yet have any other event creators and facilitators, volunteers can be handy for specific tasks like setup and cleanup. One way to encourage volunteering is to charge an admission fee to most participants, but allow those who volunteer for certain tasks to attend for free. Just be sure to have a clear agreement in advance regarding when you need them to arrive, the minimum amount of time you expect them to stay, and what tasks they're expected to do. Make known in advance the maximum number of volunteers you have room for, versus paid attendees.

Consider the Merits of Charging for Events

Asking participants to make some type of financial investment will benefit the entire group. First, if you have a tendency to give beyond what you're happily willing to give for free, this can help to avoid that. When you feel happier and more energized, participants will also feel it.

When you organize events, you're adding value for other people while also decreasing the time you have to spend on other activities, such as making money at a day job. Therefore, you shouldn't be ashamed to request compensation for your time, especially if you're hosting events frequently. Also, you're incurring some financial costs by hosting events: even little things like toilet paper and laundry detergent for washing fluff add up over time. If others sense that you find the job to be draining and costly, they'll be less likely to want to take the reins when you're ready to pass them on. If the group ceases to be sustainable, that doesn't help anyone.

Sure, in an ideal world, all the physical touch we need would always be available entirely for free, and no facilitated events would even be necessary. However, there's such an unmet need that professional cuddlers and snugglers who provide one-on-one services are even starting to crop up. Given the time, necessary level of maturity, and additional risk often assumed with such interactions, they must charge a much higher per-person hourly rate than would be sufficient for a group event. Alongside such options, which are highly valuable and a great fit for some people, snuggle parties provide a relatively affordable option for others—even if there's a fee.

As noted elsewhere, placing a monetary value on events also gives people incentive to volunteer. It also keeps frequent volunteers from feeling like they're the only ones contributing to the cause, or feeling like other participants are getting a free ride on their backs.

Finally, when people have made even a small investment of money or time, they're more likely to feel an active ownership in the group and to take things seriously. This includes making an effort to learn and follow the basic ground rules, to show up for events when they've RSVPd "yes," and to contribute to making each event as enjoyable as possible for everyone.

We tend to have a stereotype—which is sometimes true, but not always—that something offered for free is not as valuable as something with a fee. I learned this several years ago when I attempted to offer pro bono life coaching to several clients. Even one who seemed to be a serious and disciplined person failed to show up for a few rescheduled appointments in a row. Despite all my training and the value I had to offer, these clients didn't seem to treat coaching appointments as seriously as those who were gladly paying for my services. Now, I still occasionally accept a client at a lower rate, but not pro bono. If you want to attract attendees who take your events seriously, charge at least a small amount for them. Both you and your participants will be happier.

Ways to Charge While Minimizing Exclusion

There are several options for managing payment for events, and getting money to help defray costs.

If you plan to maintain a website for your group, or have a volunteer who can help you to do this, there are at least two possibilities. You can collect donations through a link on the group's site, via an online payment service. Additionally, you can find a business who wishes to sponsor the group by paying for an advertisement on the website. This can help to defray website costs, which can be substantial for some social networking and event planning sites.

If you want to charge an admissions fee for some or all events, but you prefer to avoid technology, fret not. If you trust your attendees on an honor system, the lowest-tech approach is putting out a collection jar that people simply put money into as they arrive. Leave some low-denomination bills in the jar so attendees can make themselves change if needed.

If you don't mind tinkering with the computer a bit, you can encourage people to pay online in advance using an event planning, ticketing, or payment site. A few current ones are listed in the "Additional Resources" chapter. The nice thing about this option is that it usually offers a few options for keeping track of attendees as they arrive. You can print out the attendee list or view it on a computing device. Some sites even allow attendees to print tickets or display them on their smart phone if that suits you better—although having to manage any kind of ticket is not as convenient from their end, and can discourage people who don't have as much access to technology. Chances are, you'll still have a few people who want to pay at the door; you'll have to decide whether you wish to allow that option as well.

Creating name tags for those who have paid in advance is one way to gauge who still does and doesn't need to pay at the event. Those who haven't yet paid won't have a name tag, so you'll have an obvious indicator. Just remember to disable online sales before you print the attendee list; otherwise people may pay online at the last minute after you print the list, creating confusion for you.

To encourage people to pay in advance, you can make the advance online payment a few dollars cheaper than at-the-door payment. So that you're not having to check any lists at the last minute, announce that online tickets are available until 24 hours before the event. After that, it's cash at the door only.

If you're concerned about excluding some people due to cost, you can host some events that are free of charge and others that have an admissions fee. With the free events, you can minimize your costs by providing little or no food or refreshments, encouraging others to bring things if they wish.

Alternately, you can incorporate a sliding scale recommended contribution for some or all of your events. I've seen this done a few ways. One is simply to advertise what the range is, e.g., "$10 to $15 contribution per person," and another is to state both a preferred and a limited-income cost, e.g., "$15 contribution per person, and $10 concession or limited-income contribution if necessary."

Kristen Reynolds at loving-community.com suggests basing sliding scale amounts upon one's annual income range. For example, someone who makes under $15,000 per year might pay $10 for an event, while someone who makes over $100,000 per year might pay $50. Her following cartoon illustrates this concept. This avoids scenarios where some people are investing several hours worth of earnings for an event, whereas others are investing only a fraction of an hour of earnings. Opinions may vary on this, as some individuals have worked harder than others to earn a higher income. Regardless, fairness and economic accessibility are important considerations, especially if we want snuggle parties to support broader social sustainability.

Old Way:
How Much a $65 workshop costs.

This workshop costs **8** hours of my time, plus I will need to skip breakfast for a **month**.

Well, it costs **4** hours of money. Maybe I'll skip some lattes this week.

This workshop costs **20 minutes** of my time plus I don't give up **anything**.

Reynolds 2014

Master Permaculture Gardener	Public School Teacher	Neurosurgeon
$8 per hour	**$16** per hour	**$200** per hour

New Way:
Sliding Scale for $65 workshop

Woof! 2 hours is still a lot, but I can manage.

I can afford to pay what I make in 2 hours.

I'm happy to pay what I make in 1 hour.

Reynolds 2014

Master Permaculture Gardener   Public School Teacher   Neurosurgeon

De-Stress before and after Events

While many aspects of snuggle parties are relaxing, unforeseen things sometimes occur, even if you follow every suggestion outlined earlier for simplifying logistics, recruiting volunteers, and anticipating social dynamics. For example, maybe you told someone that the RSVP list was full and they showed up with two friends anyway. Or maybe your volunteer got there half an hour late, leaving you rushing around at the last minute.

In such cases, you may find yourself going into an event with higher levels of stress. Or, afterwards you may find yourself second guessing how you handled things, wondering whether your guests noticed the hiccups and still had a good time, and so on. If you already have effective techniques for managing stress in other areas of your life, you may wish to utilize them before and after your snuggle parties as well. Some additional ideas:

- If you have a co-facilitator, ask them if they can arrive a bit earlier and stay a bit later than attendees, not just to help with logistics, but to provide emotional support. Devote a few minutes before the event sharing any fears, and communicating how the other person can provide emotional support.

- Shortly before the event, exchange a shoulder, back, or foot rub with a co-facilitator or friend.

- Devote 10 or 15 minutes after the event to a debriefing. Share with a co-facilitator or friend what you believe went well and what you wish could have gone better. If this won't work, see if a friend would be available to talk the next day.

- If you're doing an evening event, plan it to end at least an hour before your bedtime, so that you have time to unwind.

- While it may sound somewhat clichéd, few things beat getting a good night's sleep the prior evening.

- As you'll likely be busy the hour or two before the event, plan something earlier in the day to help lower your stress levels. This could include walking, jogging, sitting under a tree for half an hour, napping, treating yourself to lunch, meditating, doing yoga, cranking up a few favorite songs and dancing, or curling up to read a book you enjoy.

- If you find yourself ruminating after events, worrying about what participants actually thought, consider asking for feedback. Real-life constructive criticism may be gentler than what your imagination is capable of creating. A feedback survey can be as simple as two questions: "What did you like most about the event?" and "What would make future events more enjoyable for you?" You can print out short anonymous forms that guests fill out and drop in a jar before leaving, or you can use free online survey services. Some social networking websites have simple survey or polling capabilities built in.

- If you are the only facilitator in your local group, and you're unable to get quite the kind of support you need from your friends, consider joining an online community with resources for facilitators, such as TribalLove.net or cuddleparty.com. Even if you can't talk with someone in person, having one or more fellow facilitators to share experiences with via online forum, email, phone, or video chat can also be helpful.

Make Sure Some Events Nourish You

If you ever begin to feel like your events are meeting everyone else's needs, but not meeting your own needs, consider that not all events need to look the same. For example, if you ever start to feel burned out on hosting relatively public events, consider holding a few small and private events with friends whose presence really nourishes and recharges you. If needed, over time you can scale back your involvement with events that aren't your cup of tea, while focusing more energy on those that do. If others express continued interest in events that no longer energize you, offer to help some of them learn the facilitation ropes.

Know Your Own Comfort Zones

As you continue to host events and become more networked into the touch-positive community, your own comfort levels, preferences, and curiosity around the entire spectrum of touch may evolve. For example, as you dig beneath cultural conditioning and become more attuned to your authentic desires around non-sexual touch, you might find yourself questioning your attitudes and practices around more sexual touch as well.

It's akin to letting a domesticated cat out of the house for the first time. Initially, the cat may be perfectly happy spending most of its time in the yard just outside the house.

Eventually, it may decide to peek or hop over the fence. After that, it may decide to continue exploring further, or it may decide that its own yard already has everything it wants.

As you're evolving, you will likely encounter people with an increasingly diverse range of touch preferences. On one hand, you'll probably meet many people who are looking to increase their comfort with solely platonic touch. On the other hand, as you learn to express your own wants more confidently and effectively, people who are open to a broader range of touch may also be more comfortable sharing their preferences with you.

For example, over time you might receive invitations or inquiries regarding events of a more sexual nature. People who are well-grounded and considerate will never try to get you to do anything you're not interested in, or try to coax you after you've already said "No." Sure, as a touch-positive event facilitator, you might attract a creepy predator-type person once in a while. But in many cases when people share such preferences, they're doing so because they trust you. They're assuming that you have the ability to set your own boundaries and to simply decline if you're not interested.

You might decide that someone is just too different from you to affiliate with at all, or that they make you too uncomfortable. You might also decide that getting to know people with differences is a great opportunity to practice your communication, provided they seem respectful and you're avoiding any situations that seem unsafe. Either way is okay. Ultimately it's up to you to determine what your comfort zones are, to act in a way that respects yourself and others, and to communicate your preferences honestly and clearly.

This, in turn, will set a model for others to navigate the diverse spectrum of human touch.

Distribute Hosting Responsibilities

If hosting every event in your own home starts to feel like a hassle, don't be shy about asking others if they're willing to provide space for some events. Especially for free or almost-free events, rotating locations can help to keep any one person from feeling like they're taking on too much. You can still offer to facilitate some or all such events, but you'll be free of the burden of having to clean and declutter your own home before the event, handle any cleanup missed by volunteers after the event, and so on.

Distributing hosting responsibilities is also helpful if you want to host events that are larger than you can accommodate in your own home. As mentioned earlier under "Ideas if Space is Limited," you can charge an admission fee and offer a portion to the host as rent if no one volunteers their space for free.

13 You're Part of a Larger Movement

"I used to spend $60 per week on massage, and now I have friends with whom I can share different types of touch."

—*K. R., age 51*

Our culture is largely touch-starved as a whole, and it's important work that you're setting out to do. Hopefully you'll find others who are interested right off the bat. But even if you don't, keep the following in mind:

- You're shifting deeply-ingrained societal attitudes, one person at a time. Simply building awareness about new options, or opening up someone's mind with a glowing ember of new possibility, is an important step.

- While profound societal shifts rarely happen overnight, profound shifts in individual lives sometimes do.

- You're far from alone in your desire to create change.

- Just one event can make a huge difference.

The below account is from James "Jas" Davis, mentioned earlier. He is a founder of the group that now manages TribalLove.net, a social network site devoted to supporting heart-conscious, touch-positive communities, events, and their facilitators. It presently has more than 10,000 members worldwide, and covers the range from platonic events to events welcoming sexual energy. Jas' first experience with snuggling sparked a larger movement that later led me to discover snuggles, 10 years (almost to the date) after the first snuggle event he helped to catalyze:

My first experience of snuggling in a group was when a few friends and I created our own little snuggle puddle in the Temple of Bliss yurt at Burning Man in 2002...We weren't high or altered in any way. We simply stopped to rest and ended up in a little puppy pile. I felt so right with the world, so at peace, so complete and whole in that moment, and I remarked to my friends, "Everybody should do this...We should all snuggle more often." That idea was burned into my mind and my heart.

I came home and convinced several friends in the then-fledgling LoveTribe community to create a "Snuggle Party" on December 22nd, 2002; we called it the "Solstice Snuggle," and I believe we had about 25 folks...From that first gathering, Angel True headed up creating about six more snuggles the following year while I focused on developing a much more robust community facilitation website (all hand coded over many, many long nights)—what people would later call a social networking site.

Jas explains that a number of other people have also been instrumental in getting the group to where it currently is, and that their movement has already been through its own waxes and wanes. Even though their community as a whole hosted over 1,000 events in its first decade, and reached people in over 600 cities, they have spent the last few years developing an infrastructure to support a global touch-positive community over the longer term. Given the type of change that Jas' initial experience helped to spark, it's impossible to predict what your own snuggle events may catalyze over time.

Stara Shakti, mentioned earlier, attended a LoveTribe snuggle event at an outdoor concert in the forest. It had a profound impact upon her, and helped to inspire the creation of the group now called Oregon Touch. While she and co-founder Jack Ohana passed the reins upon moving, that group has continued to grow under new leadership. Less than two years after forming, it has attracted over 400 snugglers.

How many people in your city or town may be waiting for such a group?

And if Stara hadn't worked closely with at least two other individuals, Gabriella Cordova and Teri Chiacci, to catalyze the Ecosex Symposium that brought me to Portland a few years ago, this book would not exist. Again, it's difficult to predict what the results of even a single event will be.

Another core LoveTribe catalyst, Shanya Luther, has been raising funds for a traveling Snuggle Mobile, designed to bring nurturing platonic touch to people in a range of settings. Her team is also working on SnuggleHQ, a website to feature information on this project and various other snuggle-related resources.

Jas and his friends aren't the only ones who have already dedicated many hours to getting the word out. Marcia Baczynski and Reid Mihalko created the Cuddle Party model in 2004, and their organization has trained facilitators in a number of states. One facilitator, Monique Darling, has already thrown more than 300 cuddle parties, and another, Betty Martin, will be releasing a touch-related book.

Before any of the above, books including *Touching: The Human Significance of the Skin* (1978) and *Vitamin T: A Guide to Healthy Touch* (1991) helped to set the stage as touch pioneers like Ashley Montagu, Bob Czimbal, and Maggie Zadikov endeavored to promote awareness. Bob and Maggie continue to deliver their messages through workshops and presentations. And yet the general public is just starting to gain awareness and acceptance of important touch-related concepts today. There's still much work to do.

A number of innovative snuggle-oriented businesses have cropped up, including services that send professional snugglers to homes, and others that offer cuddling services in a business venue. Just a few examples include The Snuggle House in Madison, WI; Cuddle Up to Me in Portland, OR; Snuggle Lab in Eugene, OR; The Snuggle Buddies, covering several states in the northeastern U.S.; and The Snuggery in Rochester, NY. These businesses can provide great value to people who have an urgent need for additional touch in their lives, people who are shy about developing contacts willing to share physical touch, and people whose lifestyles leave little time to develop contacts or organize snuggle events.

At the same time, there are also many touch-starved people who cannot afford the rates that such businesses must charge to maintain a profit. So there's plenty of need for both professional snuggle services and lower-cost or amateur offerings like snuggle parties.

A few hard-working individuals have helped to spread the word through creating documentaries covering snuggle parties. There's the 10-minute video *Touch*, created by Deborah Rodney and available on YouTube, in which I make a cameo appearance alongside some of my music. There's also *Cuddle: A Documentary* by Jason O'Brien, which examines "the trend of cuddle parties and snuggle houses, cuddle therapy, and much more." Each person who watches these videos will expand their understanding about touch.

While the above people have gotten the initial ball rolling, most people you know are probably still unaware of such options. Many of them are probably experiencing loneliness and lack of touch, but don't yet know there are other ways to connect. No one person or group can reach everyone—that's where you come in. You have a personality, skill set, and life story that's uniquely suited to reach some of those people. The music inside of you is different than the music inside of anyone else, anywhere. How will your music, your unique energy, carry this exciting work forward?

14 Moving Forward

"There's a unique and profound relaxation that I experience only when I am cuddled up to three or more people. My guard drops and I feel totally safe and enfolded in my tribe."

—*S. T., age 45*

W e've covered a lot of ground, and you now have the tools you need to start creating a more touch-positive life and world. What you're doing takes courage—if it didn't, everyone would already have all the touch they need.

As mentioned earlier, start small, and seek help from a few friends if necessary. You're far from alone. For more ideas and inspiration, check out the "Additional Resources" chapter, and also visit snuggleparty.org. The website also includes information on at least one annual event you won't want to miss.

Don't be afraid to make mistakes, as it's the only way to learn and improve. I've certainly had my share of growth opportunities and learning experiences with various projects and events. When you're trying new experiences that stretch your boundaries, things won't always be perfect the first time around. To paraphrase *Vitamin T* co-author Bob Czimbal, give yourself permission to follow at least three E's:

- EXPAND
- EXPERIMENT
- EXPLORE

I believe that when you do so, you're more likely to become ENERGIZED, ENGAGED, and EXCEPTIONAL.

As mentioned earlier, you can download several useful tools at snuggleparty.org, including an example waiver form, printable ground rules, a snuggle party preparation checklist, and an example snuggle event description. Also check that site or get on the email list there for information on upcoming events you won't want to miss. If you'd like the one-on-one support of a strategic life coach as you move forward with creating your vision, learn about my coaching services at davewheitner.com.

Should you feel called to do this work more regularly or on a professional basis, there are opportunities to join a growing community of snuggle creators. CuddleParty.com provides facilitator trainings and will advertise your Cuddle Parties to their email lists. The LoveGuild (creators of LoveTribe and the Tribal Love Network) also provides more extensive snuggle facilitation training, as well as opportunities for training in a broader range of sensual, erotic, and tantric events. Their certification will provide access to additional TribalLove.net event promotion and management tools, information on additional learning opportunities, and eligibility to join a member-owned cooperative. Also see snugglehq.com for information on trainings through the LoveGuild and others.

Both Cuddle Party and the LoveGuild emphasize concepts such as teaching clear communication and boundary setting skills to participants. As your own skills grow, such communities can provide opportunities to share what you are learning, and to step into roles such as teaching and coaching others.

Once you become comfortable enough with snuggle dynamics, perhaps you'll feel even called to explore other offerings, such as one-on-one snuggle services. Much of the knowledge in this book is also applicable to such work. However, because there are additional safety considerations, I'd recommend consulting with a few people with experience in that area beforehand. Find out what steps they take to maintain a safe environment for themselves and their clients. At the very least, ask if they'd be willing to share their client agreement or waiver form, if it's not already available on their website.

If you create a snuggle event that you're really proud of, and want to share a few highlights about your experience, I'd love to hear about it! Feel free to post on the Wheitner Authentic Living page on Facebook or Google+, or email me through the contact page at davewheitner.com.

Happy snuggling!

15 Please Leave a Review

I f the knowledge in this book has been helpful to you or others, please look up *The Snuggle Party Guidebook* on the website where you purchased this book, and take a few moments to share your opinion through a review.

Just five minutes and a few sentences can help a book like this to reach dozens more people. That not only helps them directly, but enables me to continue to create important materials like this, which can take hundreds of hours to produce. That's a significant "return of good" on your investment. Many thanks in advance!

Comments on social networking sites are also greatly appreciated, including the Wheitner Authentic Living page on Facebook or my page on Google+. You're also welcome to share feedback directly with me through the contact page at davewheitner.com.

16 About the Author

Y ou can connect with Dave Wheitner through davewheitner.com, where maintains his blog, email contact page, social media page links, and other resources.

Dave guides others to create happier and more powerful lives through his life coaching practice. Raised in a blue-collar environment before attending some of the world's wealthiest schools, he has become keenly aware of cultural dynamics that impact all of us. Dave earned a B.A. in Psychology from Yale University, an M.A. in Community Counseling from Indiana University of Pennsylvania, an M.S. in Public Policy and Management from Carnegie Mellon University, and life coaching certification through the Institute for Life Coach Training. He has participated in various workshops and trainings on awareness, authenticity, sensuality, sexuality, organizational dynamics, and personal growth.

An award-winning author, Dave's other works include *Naked Idealism*, an empowerment guide for socially conscious and outside-the-box people. *More Than a Sidewalk to Sleep On* explores our relationships with gratitude and wealth, largely through the eyes of homeless individuals. A "mostly plant-based" person who embraces many but not all aspects of veganism, he's written two cookbooks. *The Global Vegan Waffle Cookbook* has tips on food-related social events, and T*he Vegan Chocolate Seduction Cookbook* blends food and sensuality. His sensual poetry appears in the anthology *Ecosexuality: When Nature Inspires the Arts of Love.* He appears in the short documentary *Touch,* along with some of his music.

Dave has created and facilitated a range of events, including snuggles with Oregon Touch. Through 15 years of co-hosting events that developed into WaffleParty.com, a celebration of conscious eating, Dave gained an appreciation for parties as social change tools. He then discovered snuggle parties during a challenging period of major life transition, and experienced their life-changing impacts. He's deeply grateful to everyone who has made this journey possible, and hopes that this book helps to carry their energy forward.

17 Additional Resources

These are not exhaustive lists; they are merely intended to get you started if you wish to explore further. Inclusion of a resource on a list does not necessarily imply my personal endorsement; they are offered merely as an educational tool. I cannot provide personal recommendations or reviews, as I do not have personal experience with all of the resources listed, and the features and offerings are subject to change.

Books on Snuggling and Touch

Czimbal, Bob and Zadikov, Maggie. *Vitamin T: A Guide to Healthy Touch*. Portland, OR: The Abundance Company, 1991. Print.

A comprehensive guide that describes various types of touch, covers helpful concepts such as leveling, and inspires further thinking about one's touch history, style, and preferences.

Grader, Rob. *The Cuddle Sutra: An Unabashed Celebration of the Ultimate Intimacy*. Sourcebook Casablanca, 2007. Print.

Includes illustrated examples of various cuddling positions.

Hess, Samantha. *Touch: The Power of Human Connection*. Fulcrum Solutions, LLC, 2014. Print.

Includes illustrated descriptions of various cuddle positions and tools such as a "Cuddle Personality Quiz" to provide a better sense of one's own touch needs.

Lynch, James. *A Cry Unheard: New Insights Into the Medical Consequences of Loneliness.* Baltimore, MD: Bancroft Press, 2000. Print.

Discusses the role that human interaction, including both physical touch and simple conversation, plays in physical health and well being.

Montagu, Ashley. *Touching: The Human Significance of the Skin.* New York: Harper Collins, 1978. Print.

Provides a well-documented, in-depth explanation of the developmental and health benefits of human touch.

Other Sources Cited in the Text

Anderson, Eric and McCormack, Mark. "Cuddling and Spooning: Heteromasculinity and Homosocial Tactility Among Student Athletes." *Men and Masculinities,* 12 Mar. 2014: 1-17. *Sage Publications.* Web. 2 July 2014.

Dominique. "4 Reasons Why, Actually, You Cannot Touch My Hair." *Disrupting Dinner Parties: Feminism for Everyone,* 12 June 2013. Web. 2 July 2014.

Dwyer, Liz. "No, You Can't Touch My Hair." *Los Angelista,* 13 Sept. 2009. Web. 1 July 2014.

Foster, Thomas A. Abstract/excerpt from "The Sexual Abuse of Black Men Under American Slavery." *Journal of the History of Sexuality, 20 (3),* Sept. 2011. *Project Muse.* Web. 1 July 2014.

Gardner, Will. "Cuddle Me, Please!" *The Portland Mercury,* 21 Sept. 2006. Web. 23 Jan. 2014.

Groshoff, David. "Trying to Queer Things Up a Little." *The Huffington Post,* 22 Feb. 2012. Web. 5 July 2014.

Johns, David Merritt. "Just Hold Me: Do Real Men Like to Cuddle?" *Slate*, 7 Dec. 2010. Web. 19 June 2014.

Reddy, Sumathi. "Little Children and Already Acting Mean: Children, Especially Girls, Withhold Friendship as a Weapon; Teaching Empathy." *The Wall Street Journal*, 26 May 2014. Web. 30 May 2014.

Resnick, Stella. *The Pleasure Zone: Why We Resist Good Feelings and How to Let Go and be Happy*. Berkeley, CA: Conari Press, 1997. Print.

Tripp, C.A. *The Homosexual Matrix*. 1975. Reprint. New York: Plume, 1987. Print.

Web Resources on Snuggling and Touch

Abundance Company, abundancecompany.com

Vitamin T co-authors Bob Czimbal and Maggie Zadikov, along with select colleagues, offer books, speaking engagements, and consulting on touch positivity, communication, relationships, and various related topics.

Cuddle Comfort, cuddlecomfort.com

Site designed for locating other nearby touch-positive individuals interested in cuddling. Allows users to create and search profiles with a range of personal characteristics, send messages, and participate in discussion forums.

Cuddle Mattress, cuddle-mattress.com

This company produces a foam mattress that has slots to accommodate arms and feet, so snugglers can remain in a broader range of positions over longer periods of time.

Cuddle Party, CuddleParty.com

This company provides training for becoming an event facilitator. The site includes information on events hosted by facilitators trained in their model.

Cuddle: The Documentary, thecuddlemovie.com/

This film by Fast Lane Productions (2014) covers a range of perspectives regarding cuddle-related events and businesses. The film maker traveled around the U.S. to interview people who have become involved in snuggling in a variety of ways.

Envision Arts Studio, envisionplay.com

Amy Baker, an art therapist, writer, and co-coordinator of Oregon Touch, is building a website and virtual community dedicated to blending creativity, collaborative play, and mindfulness practices to support each person's unique path of recovery, healing, and growth.

Kaleidoscope Community Yoga, kldyoga.org

This form of yoga incorporates a significant amount of touch and teamwork with other participants, so it's another way to become accustomed to having more touch in your life. The site includes information on a guidebook for those who wish to start a group in their area.

Loving Community, loving-community.com

Writer, illustrator, and Oregon Touch co-coordinator Kristen Reynolds provides practical thoughts on forming stable, cooperative relationships within community. The "Nurturing Touch" link on her site includes a description of her snuggle events, and many posts include her snuggly animal sketches.

Oregon Touch Meetup, meetup.com/Oregontouch/

A working example of an online group devoted to snuggle events and similar activities. Facilitators offer touch-positive events in a range of settings, with a variety of themes.

Snuggle Central (formerly The Spoon Drawer: Physical Touch Community), facebook.com/groups/161897667302168/

Posts and discussion topics include snuggle events, cuddle-related groups, businesses, and informational resources.

SnuggleHQ, snugglehq.com

Will include a range of resources on snuggling and nurturing platonic touch, including events, products, stories, and information on the traveling Snuggle Mobile.

Snuggle Party, snuggleparty.org

The website for this book includes access to printable versions of tools found in the text, links to a number of related resources, key concepts and definitions for those new to snuggling, and information on related events.

***Touch*, youtube.com/watch?v=5-ecLADiFn4**

This 10-minute video by Flying Point Moving Pictures (2013) includes footage and interviews from a snuggle event, a free hugs demonstration, and touch-positive dance. It also includes opinions on the benefits of touch and snuggling from several snuggle veterans.

"Touch Made Simple" Graphic, http://cliffnotestolife.wordpress.com/2014/01/12/touch-made-simple/

This detailed graphic by Tate Sprite offers another model for organizing the spectrum of human touch, incorporating different functions, types of connection, and levels of intimacy.

Touch Practice, touchpractice.com

This organization offers workshops and sessions designed to allow men to experience nurturing, empowering, non-sexual touch with one another more comfortably.

Tribal Love Network, TribalLove.net

Social networking and event planning site providing a range of resources for heart-conscious, touch-positive events and interaction. Resources include educational documents and group/event management tools for facilitators, the ability to create and search profiles with a range of personal characteristics, messaging, and discussion forums.

Wheitner Authentic Living, davewheitner.com

Includes a description of Dave's strategic life coaching and speaking services, blog articles on self-improvement topics including touch, books, music inspired by thought-provoking themes, photos with inspiring quotes, and links to socially conscious events.

Event Invitation and Social Networking Sites

This is a handful of sites and features available at the time of this writing. A range of approaches are available. For example, you may wish to advertise your event through multiple invitation and social networking sites, with all of them linking to a single ticketing site page.

Evite.com

Invitation-oriented site that allows for creation of event invitations, sending of invitations via email, and tracking of RSVP's.

Facebook.com

Social networking site that allows for creation of group and event pages, invitation of Facebook users to events, and tracking of RSVP's.

Google+

Social networking site that allows for creation of events, invitation of Google+ users to events, creation of "communities" of users with similar interests, and tracking of RSVP's

Meetup.com

Social networking site established specifically for creating groups with shared interests, organizing events, and locating local events that match one's interests.

Nextdoor.com

Social networking site that can be used to promote events to people in your neighborhood. It enables you to communicate with others verified as living nearby, but you can choose to hide your specific address in your profile.

Punchbowl.com

Invitation-oriented site that offers a guided process for planning a party, sending out invitations, tracking RSVP's, and following up with guests.

TribalLove.net

Social networking site established specifically for connecting people around heart-centered and touch-positive events, spanning the full range from platonic to erotic. Includes social networking and event organizing tools.

Event Ticketing and Payment Sites

These sites can be useful if you wish to host a paid event, or if you host a free event and want to require reservations of "tickets" to get a more accurate and consolidated RSVP count. They usually charge some type of per-ticket fee for non-free events, and include different types of integration with social networking sites.

brownpapertickets.com

eventbrite.com

ticketbud.com

ticketriver.com

Resources for More Intimate and Erotic Touch

The professionals and organizations below cover a range of services and offerings: coaching or customized training from experienced facilitators; events with different levels of erotic touch; events with unclothed but not necessarily erotic touch; online tools, training, and support for event facilitators; trainings and credentialing for current and aspiring sex educators; and trainings on integrating sensuality and sexuality with spiritual practices.

Abundance Company, abundancecompany.com

American Association of Sexuality Educators, Counselors, and Therapists, aasect.org

Betty Martin, bettymartin.org

The Body Electric School, thebodyelectricschool.com

Divine Feminine Institute, divine-feminine.com

Human Awareness Institute, hai.org

OneTaste Orgasmic Meditation, OneTaste.us

Reid Mihalko, reidaboutsex.com

Sex Positive World, sexpositiveworld.org

Source School of Tantra Yoga, sourcetantra.com

Touch Practice, touchpractice.com

Tribal Love Network, triballove.net

18 Acknowledgments

Thanks to the many wonderful individuals and groups whose events I have attended, those with whom I have facilitated events, and those who have shared useful knowledge and insights with me through various conversations and books. I'm deeply grateful for those who have changed my life in ways that have catalyzed valuable learning experiences and realizations, too numerous to list in entirety here.

Thanks also to those who provided the anonymous "how snuggling has impacted my life" quotes that appear throughout the text.

Amy Baker, Bob Czimbal, James "Jas" Davis, Megan Lilah Martin, Kristen Reynolds, Ashley "Jack" Ohana, Stara Shakti, and Maggie Zadikov provided significant amounts of input, including direct and indirect comments on drafts.

Others to whom I'm indebted include but are not limited to: Serena Anderlini D'Onofrio, Authentic Portland, Bruce Bartlett, Brian Bloom, John Brennan, David Cates, Teri Ciacchi, Gabriella Cordova, Sally Dubats, Carolyn Elliott, Jenny Ferry, Monica Gaydos, Lisa Gorlin, Stephen Horvath, Brian Houghton, Sherry Houghton, Jen Joy, Savanna Joy, Albert Kaufman, Avi Klepper, The LoveGuild and Tribal Love Network, Shanya "Torch" Luther, Mehdi Mojtabavi, Mt. Tabor Divorce Support Group, Andrea Nelken, Network for a New Culture, Eleanor O'Brien, Oregon Touch, The Pittsburgh Alternative Relationship Meetup, the Portland Ecstatic Dance Community, Portland Sacred Tantra Club and its puja facilitators, the Portland Salon Group, John Raymond, Cliff Rees, Kelly Rees, Michael Rios, Abby Samuels, Ed Seidenberg, Evan Silverman, Sex-Positive Portland, Snuggle Lab, Maren Souders, Sarah Taub, and Debra and Gary Wheitner. And all of my teachers, instructors, and mentors.

I'm deeply grateful for the higher power that connects all of us on this journey, however you may perceive it.

19 Endnotes

1 Adapted from a definition provided by Kristen Reynolds, and comments from Jas Davis.

2 Gardner (2006), Johns (2010), and Jas Davis.

3 LoveTribe, for example, uses terms such as "Romps" and "Eros Parties" for events that allow erotic energy and touch.

4 Montagu (1978), Lynch (2000).

5 Montagu (1978).

6 Lynch (2000).

7 Reddy (2014). Thanks to Danielle Goldman for making me aware of this article.

8 Resnick (1997).

9 I'm very grateful to Alan Kazdin for his many influential lectures at Yale, alongside his writing.

10 For more on the seemingly paradoxical but complementary relationship between independence/differentiation and closeness/romantic attraction, see *Mating in Captivity* by Esther Perel or *Intimacy and Desire* by David Schnarch.

11 Exceptions may include individuals who are asexual, or who are otherwise no longer interested in sex at all due to medical or other reasons.

12 Thanks to Kristen Reynolds for the concept of the radical nature of increasing platonic touch.

13 Adapted from a definition provided by Kristen Reynolds, and comments from Jas Davis.

14 Thanks to Bob Czimbal and Maggie Zadikov for this sign, also adopted in other physically interactive settings such as Portland's ecstatic dance and contact improvisational dance communities.

15 See *Vitamin T: A Guide to Healthy Touch* for more depth on leveling. Bob Czimbal, Maggie Zadikov, Jas Davis, and LoveTribe have been instrumental in spreading awareness of this concept.

16 Thanks to Kristen Reynolds for this additional point.

17 Thanks to Kristen Reynolds for this point.

18 Courtesy of Jas Davis; also available at TribalLove.net.

19 See *Vitamin T: A Guide to Healthy Touch* for additional thoughts on touch histories.

20 Thanks to Amy Baker for this idea.

21 I had a lot of fun co-facilitating a movie night with Oregon Touch, and LoveTribe has organized "Puppy Pile Movie Nights."

22 Thanks to Jas Davis and LoveTribe for this idea.

23 Thanks to Jas Davis for additional thoughts on highly portable gym mats. As of this writing, several online vendors offer 2'x6' mats, between 1" and 2" thick, that can be folded to 2'x2' or 2'x3' with a handle.

24 Thanks to Mehdi Mojtabavi for taking the time to speak with me about his creation, described at cuddle-mattress.com.

25 Thanks to Megan Lilah Martin for this idea.

26 Thanks to Jas Davis, Jen Joy, and Stara Shakti for the candle-in-fireplace idea.

27 Thanks to Jas Davis for additional thoughts on food and beverage.

28 Thanks to Jas Davis for additional thoughts on venues.

29 Thanks to Bob Czimbal for generating the analogy that I've expounded upon here.

30 As mentioned earlier, Oregon Touch presently excludes snuggles from its orientation events. Thanks to them for the reasoning around this.

31 LoveGuild is the organization that oversees facilitator trainings for events bearing the LoveTribe brand.

32 As it was difficult to track down original sources of the games, especially as they often evolve, I've footnoted individuals whose workshops featured such a game or a variation of it.

33 Thanks to David Cates for initially introducing me to this concept, which I've since experienced at a few events. Thanks also to Gabriella Cordova, Teri Ciacchi, Stara Shakti, and others for organizing the Ecosex Symposium where I had the chance to learn from many skilled facilitators.

34 Thanks to Authentic Portland and to Network for a New Culture East for modeling this game in a wonderfully fun way. I do not know the game's origins, or how much it has evolved.

35 In the initial release of this book, this game was called "Sociometric Circle."

36 I've experienced variations on this exercise at several events, including those facilitated by Bob Czimbal and Maggie Zadikov, and Portland's Sacred Tantra Club.

37 See *Vitamin T: A Guide to Healthy Touch* for additional depth on leveling. Bob Czimbal and Maggie Zadikov, along with Jas Davis and LoveTribe, have been instrumental in spreading awareness of this concept.

38 Jas Davis and LoveTribe have been instrumental in developing the term *re-leveling*, building upon the original concept of leveling as described in *Vitamin T*. Thanks also to Kristen Reynolds for her thoughts on this concept.

39 Thanks to Stara Shakti, Ashley "Jack" Ohana, and Oregon Touch for demonstrating the value of this.

40 I've experienced variations on this exercise at several events, including those facilitated by Bob Czimbal and Maggie Zadikov, Portland's Sacred Tantra Club, and Oregon Touch.

41 Thanks to Jas Davis for this idea.

42 Thanks to Megan Lilah Martin for helping me to clarify some thoughts on this.

43 Thanks to Jas Davis for this.

44 Thanks to Kristen Reynolds for the term *snuggle ambassador*.

45 The Q and A in LGBTQIA sometimes also refer to *questioning* and *ally*. See pflag.org and Groshoff (2012) for more information on the increasing use of *queer* as an umbrella term for all of these categories. While many people within the LGBTQIA community now prefer it, some still reject it due to its history as a derogatory term. Also, while some definitions of homophobia seem to include transphobia, I include both terms here to promote awareness since there are some differences.

46 Anderson and McCormack (2014).

47 Tripp, C.A. (1975).

48 A few individuals suggested that I use the terms *gender imbalance* and *gender balancing* to avoid confusion, as these terms are already popularly used. However, *gender* also refers to non-biological characteristics such as self-perceived identity and gender role behaviors, whereas issues related to balancing seem to revolve largely around biological sex. Therefore, I decided to use the technically preferred terminology of *sex* to refer to biological sex. For one detailed illustration designed to convey elements of gender identity, see the "Genderbread Person" graphic viewable at itspronouncedmetrosexual.com.

49 Thanks to Bob Czimbal for his thoughts on this.

50 From the National Symposium on Neurodiversity, as cited at wikipedia.org.

51 There is still some debate over whether Asperger's should be its own separate diagnosis, rather than being included on the "Autism Spectrum Disorder." So individuals may vary on what label they personally prefer—including whether they accept the term *disorder*.

52 Thanks to Kristen Reynolds for pointing out the importance of including this section.

53 Foster (2011).

54 Dominique (2013).

55 Reprinted with author's permission.

56 Thanks to Bob Czimbal and Kristen Reynolds for provoking thought on this topic, which included a discussion on the distinction between *bisensuality* and *bisexuality*.

57 Going a bit deeper with this, there's also a distinction between sensuality and romantic orientation. This is worth noting because the latter does not always align with sexual orientation. An example is a person who is heteroromantic and asexual. They enjoy being romantic with members of the other sex, but don't feel the need to have sex with anyone. At the same time, they may be pansensual, enjoying activities like snuggling with everyone.

58 Thanks to Bob Czimbal and Kristen Reynolds for provoking thought on this topic.

59 Given limited space, I chose examples of heterosexual men and women here because on average, individuals who fit within a

cultural majority are less likely to have given thought to related dynamics. This is often simply because the impacts upon them are not as immediately obvious. I am not suggesting that others are immune from such dynamics.

60 As noted earlier, I chose to use the technically preferred term *sex* to refer to biological sex, even though the term *gender balancing* is often used.

61 Thanks to Oregon Touch for this idea.

62 There are some individuals who believe that little or no hierarchy should exist among one's relationships, but this section speaks to the majority of people who prefer relationships where primary partners prioritize one another.

63 Thanks to Bob Czimbal for this idea.

64 LoveTribe and the LoveGuild originally created the form from which most of these ideas were derived. I've made slight modifications including input from Snuggle Lab. Thanks to Shanya Luther and Snuggle Lab for inspiring some thoughts on this section. Check TribalLove.net, snuggleparty.org, and snugglehq.com for additional waiver language.

65 For events where reporters or other media will be present, it's very important to get clear consent from everyone in attendance. I recommend having a media release form for attendees to sign that outlines the way in which attendees' images, statements, etc., may appear in the media, just for that specific event. Potential attendees should also be notified in advance that media will be present, preferably at the time the event is announced.

66 Thanks to Lisa Gorlin and Tate Sprite for inspiring some of my thinking on these topics. Tate Sprite's detailed "Touch Made Simple" graphic at http://cliffnotestolife.wordpress.com /2014/01/12/touch-made-simple/ offers another approach to organizing types of touch, where more "intimate" touch doesn't necessarily equate to more sexual touch.

67 At the time of this writing, descriptions of their "Levels of Possibility" are accessible through the "pages" link at their website, http://www.meetup.com/sexpositivepdx/. However, their use of terms such as *sensual* may differ from the definitions in this book.

11992109R00125

Made in the USA
Monee, IL
20 September 2019